W9-BTE-701

Handbook for Conducting School Climate Improvement Projects

by

Eugene Howard, Bruce Howell,
and Edward Brainard

The PHI DELTA KAPPA EDUCATIONAL FOUNDATION

Bloomington, Indiana

Cover design by Peg Caudell

Library of Congress Catalog Card Number 87-61793
ISBN 0-87367-797-8
Copyright © 1987 by the Phi Delta Kappa Educational Foundation
Bloomington, Indiana

Table of Contents

Preface

This book is about school climate — how it is defined and how climate studies can be implemented. An earlier version, *School Climate Improvement: A Challenge to the School Administrator,* published in 1974 by Phi Delta Kappa, familiarized educators with factors about school climate that had been identified through nearly five years of deliberations by associates of CFK, Ltd., a philanthropic foundation dedicated to the improvement of educational leadership and sponsored by the late Charles F. Kettering II.

In the early 1970s research on school climate was in its initial stages; now the term *school climate* is used widely in the literature on school improvement. Volumes have been written, and many projects have been initiated — all in the name of school climate improvement. With the experience gained over more than a decade, the authors saw the need for an expanded and refined publication that would serve as a basic reference for anyone interested in school climate improvement. Therefore, they proceeded with this new publication with the objectives of 1) creating an operational definition of school climate, 2) outlining a sequential procedure for implementing school climate activities, and 3) emphasizing the continuing leadership role necessary to improve the climate in a school.

The three authors bring both common and unique backgrounds to the development of this publication. All three were members of CFK,

1

Ltd., and subsequently have been active in the Collegial Association for the Development and Renewal of Educators (CADRE), the organization that superseded CFK in 1974. All have published on the topic, have served as consultants, and have administered programs that enhance school climate. However, each brings a unique perspective to the topic.

Eugene Howard serves in the Planning and Evaluation Unit of the Colorado Department of Education. He is recognized as a national authority on implementation of school climate activities. Howard articulates the steps necessary for initiating, implementing, and evaluating school climate activities.

D. Bruce Howell synthesizes the experiences of the many superb educators involved with CFK-CADRE, whose contributions are woven into this text. As a former city superintendent and now professor of educational administration at University of Tulsa, he is committed to the pragmatic leadership needed to make school climate improvement operational.

Edward Brainard, currently an assistant superintendent in Aurora, Colorado, served as president of CFK, Ltd. from 1967 until 1974. Brainard's task has been to define school climate, drawing on his practical experiences, and then to apply the definition to current trends in education.

During the two decades that the concept of school climate has been seriously studied, clearer definitions and more practical processes have emerged. The authors believe this text synthesizes the best from both theorists and practitioners who have been working to improve the schools.

Introduction

The way to improve education is through a healthy environment at each school.
—John Goodlad, speaking in Denver, 17 January 1986

"Sunset Ridge is a much better school than it used to be. Pupils are happier, more self-confident, less alienated. They are learning more than their predecessors. Parents are involved and enthusiastic, and staff members feel positive about the work. Morale is high." In these few words Mary Lou Zarlengo, principal of Sunset Ridge School in Westminster, Colorado, gives a summary of the results achieved by one school, which contains the two goals that thoughtful educators have in mind when they study a school's climate for learning. The first goal concerns productivity, such as academic achievement. The second goal is satisfaction, such as high morale. Productivity and satisfaction are timeless goals of any school. They go hand in hand. No school can succeed without, to some degree, achieving both goals.

This book is about practical ways to improve a school's climate by increasing both productivity and satisfaction concurrently. This book will provide answers to six essential questions about school climate:

1. In practice, what is an effective school climate?
2. What does a good climate look like?
3. What instructional conditions must exist?

3

4. How can a school organization be efficient and accountable for its learning program and, at the same time, still be centrally concerned with people?
5. How can educators determine the quality of a school's climate? How can they measure it?
6. How can educators provide leadership to improve the learning environment?

Chapter 1
Defining School Climate

A school's climate is its atmosphere for learning. It includes the feelings people have about school and whether it is a place where learning can occur. A positive climate makes a school a place where both staff and students want to spend a substantial portion of their time; it is a good place to be.

Whenever educators or parents visit a school for the first time, it is common to hear remarks about the school's climate. A typical observation is, "This school has a good atmosphere," or "This school has a good feeling." What criteria do educators and parents use when making a judgment about a school's climate? What factors do they have in mind when describing the dimensions of school climate? If asked, they might offer some vague explanation; and if pressed, they are likely to respond with some positive or negative expression of general feelings. The purpose of this chapter is to translate those vague explanations and general feelings into specific factors that determine a school's climate. Once identified, then school leaders have a basis for improving a school's climate.

In the following sections, we shall identify: 1) the overarching goals of school climate improvement, 2) the basic human needs that school climate must address, 3) the factors that make up a school's climate and determine its quality, and 4) the elements of a school's operation that contribute to positive climate.

Goals of School Climate Improvement

The two paramount goals of school climate improvement certainly are not new; they always have been part of the fabric of American public education. These two goals are *productivity* and *satisfaction*.

The goal of productivity means that the school provides a wholesome, stimulating, and productive learning environment conducive to the academic and personal growth of students. Productivity includes such characteristics as achieving basic skills, developing an expanding knowledge base, and using inquiry and problem-solving processes.

The goal of satisfaction means that the school provides a pleasant and satisfying environment within which young people can work. Satisfaction includes such factors as a sense of personal worth, enjoying school, and success from participation in worthwhile activities.

A corollary of these two paramount goals for young people is providing a satisfying and productive environment for adults in the school community: teachers and other staff members, the principal, and parents.

Basic Human Needs that School Climate Must Address

If a school is to be productive and satisfying, it must fulfill basic human needs of students, faculty, and administrators. No school has a wholesome climate unless it is providing its students and faculty with these essentials:

Physiological Needs. These pertain to the school's physical plant and include heat, light, and relatively uncrowded conditions.

Safety Needs. These pertain to safety from such potential hazards as fire and to security from physical and psychological abuse or assault from others in or around the school.

Acceptance and Friendship Needs. These pertain to positive relationships with other students, faculty, and administrators.

Achievement and Recognition Needs. These pertain to the recognition of one's successful endeavors in the school.

Needs to Maximize One's Potential. These pertain to personal goals to achieve at the highest possible level.

Factors in School Climate

If you walked into a school building and tried to gain a sense of its prevailing climate, what would you look for? What elements would you consider in assessing its positive or negative climate? At least eight factors contribute to a school's climate and determine its quality. There should be evidence of:

1. *Continuous Academic and Social Growth*. Each student is developing academically, socially, and physically in skills and knowledge. Faculty, too, are improving their skills and knowledge with regard to their particular assignments and as cooperative members of the education team. Effective schools research points out that successful schools operate in a climate in which the professional staff hold high expectations for their students. They believe their students can learn, and they are committed to making sure that students do learn. In effective schools, staff are optimistic about their ability to influence student achievement. Students believe their accomplishments result from how hard they work (Robinson 1985).

2. *Respect*. Students see themselves as persons of worth; their ideas are respected. Teachers and administrators feel the same way. School is a place where individuals have self-esteem, are considerate, and appreciate others. An atmosphere of mutual respect prevails.

3. *Trust*. Trust is having confidence that others can be counted on to do what they say they will do; they have integrity.

4. *High Morale*. In a school with high morale, people feel good about what is happening. They are willing to perform assigned tasks; they are confident and cheerful. Self-discipline is the mode. A defeatest attitude does not exist.

5. *Cohesiveness*. This quality is manifested by a person's attraction to the school. It is often called school spirit or esprit de corps. People feel a sense of belonging to the school. They want to stay with it and exert their influence on it in collaboration with others.

6. *Opportunities for Input*. Not everyone can be involved in making the important decisions required in running a school's programs. But every person wants the opportunity to contribute ideas and know they have been considered. When people feel they have no voice, it diminishes their self-esteem and deprives the school of their influence.

7. *School Renewal*. The school is self-renewing; it is growing, developing, and changing. Research on effective schools indicates that in such schools the staff is confident of their ability to change, improve, and manage the learning environment. There is an atmosphere conducive to program improvement (Robinson 1985).

8. *Caring*. Individuals in the school feel that some other person or persons are concerned about them. People are interested in each other. Teachers feel that the principal cares about them. The principal

knows that the staff understands the pressures of the job and will help if they can. "Researchers found an atmosphere of cooperation and caring in effective schools. Some researchers actually describe it as a family-type atmosphere with a staff focused on student needs, working cooperatively within the framework of a well-managed organization" (Robinson 1985).

It is these eight factors that determine the quality of a school's climate for learning. They also determine the success a school will have in achieving the goals of productivity and satisfaction. But there also are indicators of negative school climate. Below is a list of symptoms of climate problems in a school. Are any of these problems in your school?

_____ High student absenteeism
_____ High frequency of student discipline problems
_____ Weak student government
_____ Student cliques
_____ High faculty absenteeism
_____ Negative discussion in faculty lounges
_____ Crowded conditions
_____ Students feeling lost because the school is too large
_____ Vandalism
_____ Student unrest
_____ Poor school spirit
_____ Poor community image of the school
_____ Faculty cliques
_____ Theft from lockers
_____ High student dropout rate
_____ Large numbers of underachieving students
_____ Low staff morale
_____ Passive students
_____ Faculty apathy
_____ Supplies and equipment unavailable when needed
_____ Poor image of the school by staff
_____ Dislike of students by some faculty members
_____ Students for whom school has little purpose
_____ High incidence of suspensions and expulsions

Determinants of School Climate Improvement

Simply identifying the factors associated with a healthy school climate is not sufficient for initiating a climate improvement program. The factors of trust, respect, cohesiveness, caring, opportunities for input, high morale, and school renewal are achieved as a result of specific practices and programs in a school's operations. Following are descriptions of 18 determinants of the quality of a school's climate. The determinants fall into three categories: program, process, and material.

Program Determinants

1. *Opportunities for active learning* in which students are totally involved and are able to demonstrate an ability to use their knowledge and skills.

2. *Individualized performance expectations* that are reasonable, flexible, and take into account individual differences. Students are frequently encouraged to set their own performance goals.

3. *Varied learning environments* that avoid a single, standard mode of instruction and that use different grouping arrangements.

4. *Flexible curriculum and extracurricular activities* that provide a wide range of content options for learners. It is not assumed that all learners in a group have the same content needs or that all will learn at the same rate. Extracurricular activities are offered to serve all students.

5. *Support and structure appropriate to the learner's maturity* whereby the school designs its programs and sets its requirements so they are consistent with the intellectual, social, and physical characteristics of the learner. Faculty are aware of and apply the principles of child and adolescent growth and development.

6. *Rules cooperatively determined* involving both faculty and students in developing clearly stated rules and regulations, which are viewed as reasonable and desirable by those affected. Research on effective schools shows that in high achieving schools discipline policies are clear, firm, and consistent. School regulations and penalties are subjected to a periodic review and are responsive to teacher and student input. In addition, these schools help students understand how expected school behavior transfers to behavior outside of school (Robinson 1985).

7. *Varied reward systems* that reinforce positive behavior. The school provides a variety of ways in which students and teachers can receive recognition.

Process Determinants

8. *Problem-solving ability* whereby skills are developed in order to reach effective solutions to problems. There are well-developed procedures for identifying problems, for inventing solutions, for implement-

ing them, and for evaluating their effectiveness. Problem-solving ability is a characteristic of effective schools (Robinson 1985).

9. *Improvement of school goals* whereby goals are clearly stated and understood by students, parents, and faculty. Goals serve as reference points for making decisions, organizing school improvement projects, and guiding day-to-day operations. Students, staff, and administrators are encouraged to develop personal goals related to school work.

10. *Identifying and working with conflicts* in a manner that recognizes that conflict is natural; it occurs within individuals, between them, and between groups. Conflict need not be a problem unless it is allowed to fester. In a favorable climate, conflict is approached in a positive way with staff members involved in helping to resolve the issue (Robinson 1985).

11. *Effective communications* that enhance interpersonal relationships among and between faculty, students, and parents. There is emphasis on active listening. In studies of effective schools, researchers found that when there was effective communication between teachers and principals, teachers were more satisfied with their working relationships with their principal and had more opportunities for staff input in decision making (Robinson 1985).

12. *Involvement in decision making* whereby the opportunity to improve the school exists for students, faculty, interested parents, and others. Persons affected by a decision have an opportunity to provide input. Decisions are based on adequate information, and decision-making processes are clearly specified and understood by all. A variety of decision-making models are used, and the entire process is reviewed periodically for effectiveness and efficiency.

13. *Autonomy with accountability* whereby there is a balance between being independent and self-governing and being responsible for achieving agreed-on goals and objectives. Autonomy with accountability is accepted by students, staff, and the school as a corporate body.

14. *Effective teaching-learning strategies* whereby goals for teaching-learning are clearly stated, and faculty seek evaluative feedback from students and peers. Teachers recognize that students have varied learning styles and employ methods that are compatible with these styles as well as with student maturity. Students have opportunities to choose from a variety of learning activities.

15. *Ability to plan for the future,* which involves both immediate and long-range planning. The staff analyzes the general course of the school's program and plans desirable changes in its programs and ser-

vices. The staff uses planning skills to project conditions as they and their clientele want them to be.

Material Determinants

16. *Adequate resources* that support faculty and students with instructional material centers/libraries, laboratories, suitable furniture, textbooks and other instructional materials, and expendable supplies.

17. *Supportive and efficient logistical system,* which helps people achieve school goals and enhances morale. Established procedures enable staff to acquire needed materials quickly. The system provides quality services in such areas as student scheduling, custodial and secretarial services, purchasing, budgeting, and accounting. All staff know what they can and cannot expect of the school's logistical system.

18. *Suitability of school plant,* which can be modified as program needs change. The building decor is attractive in terms of color, furniture arrangement, and displays of student work. According to the Educational Research Service report on effective schools:

> Many low achieving schools actually had more modern and better-equipped school plants than did high achieving schools. The important element was that, even though the effective schools in some cases were old, they were clean, well maintained, and often well landscaped.
>
> Researchers found unsuccessful schools to have more litter, graffiti, and vandalism. The researchers found a sense of quiet pride in high achieving schools and a sense of caring that was reflected in the positive physical appearance of the school. (Robinson 1985)

Taken as a group, the 18 elements listed above are the major determinants of the quality of a school's atmosphere for learning. Using these 18 determinants, a school can organize improvement projects that will result in a more desirable school climate.

School Climate Improvement: A Case Study

How long does it take to create an excellent school? According to Hank Gallina, principal of El Camino School in Lompoc, California, it can be done in seven years. At least that's how long Hank and his staff have been working systematically on school improvement. The results have been impressive. Achievement, as measured by the California Test of Basic Skills, has risen substantially, even though most of the children in the school are from low-income families whose first language is not English. Discipline referrals to the office, once frequent,

11

are now rare; vandalism and graffiti have almost been eliminated; and pupil absenteeism has been reduced from 40% to 10%. The use of obscene language by pupils, once a major problem, has almost been eliminated (Howard 1985).

How did Gallina change his school around? He began by becoming familiar with the work that had been done in measuring and improving school climate and concluded that it was time to take a close look at his school's climate. He did this by using the CFK, Ltd., School Climate Profile, an instrument for diagnosing the strengths and weaknesses of climate (see Appendix B).

The results were generally positive; morale and trust, two key climate factors, were seen as strengths. Active learning and support and structure (for pupils) were also program strengths. However, three process determinants — communications, problem solving, and shared decision making — were clearly perceived as problems. This information was shared with his staff, who discussed a variety of ways to improve the three problem determinants. Then, following the staff meeting, a smaller group of staff met with Gallina to develop some preliminary plans. A year later, the School Climate Profile was administered for the second time; and it showed that in one year the school's climate had improved significantly.

What has Gallina learned from his experience at El Camino? "First of all," he says, "central office administrators' and board members' support for change of this magnitude is absolutely essential. They have to know what is happening and why. The school's improvement efforts have to be congruent with the overall direction in which the district is moving." Throughout the total process, Gallina and his staff have benefited from strong support from the central office and the board of education.

"We also learned," says Gallina, "about the importance of a strong staff development program that clearly supports the improvement goals. The pacing of change was carefully controlled so that the faculty were expected to change their teaching styles gradually, as the training proceeded. Teachers were given time to grow and to experiment."

Gallina also learned the importance of involving the staff in decision-making and planning processes. He does not believe that shared governance erodes the authority of the principal. "What happens," he says, "is that the principal's power base is broadened. The principal has a previously agreed-on structure and process for gaining support for new ideas. The power base no longer rests with just the principal and a few others. The base is with the total staff."

Gallina and his staff learned about the importance of a school's climate as a precondition for excellence. The El Camino staff directed their improvement efforts toward a variety of program and process determinants that had been identified by using the School Climate Profile. They learned how improving the school's climate can result in improved learner satisfaction and achievement. "And that," says Hank Gallina, "is the bottom line."

Any school can do what Hank Gallina and his staff did at El Camino. The remainder of this book provides detailed procedures for conducting climate studies that can lead to school improvement.

References

Howard, Eugene. *School Climate Improvement: Leadership and Progress.* Aurora, Colo.: CADRE Publications, 1985.

Robinson, Glen E. *Effective Schools Research: A Guide to School Development.* Washington, D.C.: Educational Research Service, 1985.

Chapter 2
Implementing School Climate Improvement
A PROCESS THAT WORKS

In a recent study of five highly successful climate improvement projects, Howard (1985) identified an eight-step process common to all:

1. Appoint a steering committee or management team with leadership responsibilities.
2. Collect baseline data regarding climate symptoms.
3. Conduct awareness-raising activities so that parents, students, and staff are informed about the rationale for the project and the process to be followed.
4. Conduct an assessment of the school's climate.
5. Identify improvement priorities and develop action plans for improvement activities.
6. Organize task forces to accomplish the tasks identified in the action plans.
7. Coordinate the work of the task forces.
8. Evaluate the overall impact of the climate improvement effort and report the results.

The eight steps are described briefly below.

Step 1: Appoint a School Improvement Management Team (SIMT). The School Improvement Management Team oversees the school improvement process; provides leadership and support to the task forces;

obtains and maintains faculty, student, and parent support; and assesses the project's outcomes. Interested parents, students, and staff members serve on this team.

Step 2: Collect Baseline Data. Once appointed, the first task of the SIMT is to collect baseline data so that the impact of the improvement project can be measured over time. The essential question to be answered with the baseline data is: To what extent are symptoms of a quality climate apparent in the school? Data relating to this question may be obtained from assessments of pupil and staff morale, from assessments of climate factors, and from school records. Much of this data already is available in most schools. The SIMT has the task of gathering it, summarizing it, and ensuring its accuracy. For example, the SIMT may decide to gather data related to five or six of the following symptoms of school climate:

- Achievement
- Daily attendance of faculty and students
- Attendance at school-sponsored activities
- Library usage
- Percentage of students earning high and low or failing grades
- Vandalism incidents and costs (while school is in session)
- Discipline referrals (number and seriousness of offenses)
- Faculty turnover
- Drug and alcohol abuse statistics
- Suspensions (in-school and out-of-school)
- Dropouts (high school)

Step 3: Raise the Awareness Level of Faculty, Students, and Parents. Through a series of awareness-raising workshops and other activities, faculty, students, and parents learn about the climate improvement project and become convinced that an organized plan for improvement would benefit their school. Two useful activities are visiting other schools that have successful improvement programs and participating in a visiting team to conduct a climate assessment of another school.

Step 4: Assess the School's Climate. A climate assessment may be done by using an instrument designed for this purpose (see appendices) or by using a visiting assessment team. The assessment will identify those determinants that are positively or negatively affecting the school's climate. Parents, students, and the total school staff are actively involved in this process. Assessment results are analyzed, interpreted, and communicated to faculty, students, and parents.

Step 5: Brainstorm, Prioritize, and Plan. At a workshop organized for this purpose, faculty, parent, and student leaders use assessment information as a basis to brainstorm ideas on promising practices for improving the school's climate, and then to prioritize the ideas for an action plan. Usually a group chooses from one to five determinants on which to work.

Step 6: Form Task Forces. The SIMT forms from one to five task forces, one for each determinant identified as a priority. Each task force is given a charge from the SIMT to initiate activities, projects, and programs to influence positively one of the climate determinants. Task forces may be sponsored by faculty, by a parent organization, or by the student council. Each task force leader is also a member of the SIMT.

Step 7: Manage Task Forces. The SIMT and the principal facilitate and support the work of the task forces. Task force leaders report progress periodically to the principal, to the SIMT, to the staff, and to parent and student groups as appropriate.

Step 8: Conduct an Evaluation. The SIMT collects, interprets, and reports data regarding the extent to which the school's climate has been improved. The instruments and procedures used are the same as those used to collect the baseline data (Step 2).

The Eight-Step Process: A Positive Approach

The process described above differs from traditional approaches to school improvement in that the focus is on positive aspects of a school's climate rather than on its problems. The traditional approach to school improvement is to identify problems and then attempt to solve them. Such an approach can result in improvement; however, it will not result in excellence. Excellence comes by making what is working well work even better and by spreading successful practice.

The eight-step process does not ignore problems. In fact, one of the determinants of climate is concerned with the effective functioning of problem-solving processes. However, the eight-step process is not a traditional problem-solving approach; rather, it is a positive approach designed to identify and strengthen success.

16

In this chapter we have described the eight-step process and an organizational structure to implement school climate improvement. The next five chapters will provide detailed information on how to build this organizational structure and manage the eight-step process.

References

Howard, Eugene R. *School Climate Improvement: Leadership and Process.* Aurora, Colo.: CADRE Publications, 1985.

Chapter 3

Getting Ready for Climate Improvement
STEPS 1, 2, AND 3

Climate improvement projects, if done properly, require a lot of work. There is more than can be accomplished by just the principal and a few designated leaders. Tasks must be defined and delegated.

Step 1: Appoint the School Improvement Management Team

The first step in launching a schoolwide climate improvement program is the formation of a planning and coordinating group, which we call the School Improvement Management Team (SIMT). This is not an advisory group that simply studies a problem and then makes recommendations for others to carry out. This is a working group that, together with the principal, plans and coordinates the climate improvement activities in the school.

This team should not be the same as the principal's administrative cabinet. Rather, it should be composed of faculty, parents, and students who are convinced that the school should be a more caring, trusting, and cohesive place. They should have talents to contribute and should be willing to work to make the school a better place for everyone. At the outset, team members may have to be recruited; later, volunteers might be accepted. A suggested composition of the team might include:

- one or two counselors or social workers who are familiar with the characteristics of the students and the community and who understand the clique structure of the school;

18

- two or three teachers and two or three parents who believe that climate improvement is a promising approach to improving the school's quality;
- two or three student leaders; and
- the principal, who serves as the team's specialist in organization and who provides overall leadership.

Prior to the first SIMT meeting, the principal should prepare a written Statement of Purpose, informing the team of what it is expected to accomplish. A sample Statement of Purpose appears in Figure 3.1.

Figure 3.1

TO: School Climate Improvement Management Team
FROM: Margaret Glasgow, Principal, Washington School
SUBJECT: Statement of Purpose (First Draft)

The School Climate Improvement Management Team is the Washington School's planning and coordinating group for all major climate improvement projects. The team is charged with accomplishing the following tasks:

1. Conducting a study of the school climate improvement process so that committee members become knowledgeable about what climate is and how it can be assessed.
2. Collecting baseline data on the extent to which climate is already positive in the school.
3. Developing a library of materials on climate improvement, including descriptions of promising practices in other schools.
4. Visiting other schools engaged in schoolwide climate improvement programs.
5. Planning and conducting information-sharing sessions with parent, faculty, and student groups.
6. Conducting an assessment of the climate of Washington School and interpreting the results of that assessment to parents, staff, and students.
7. Identifying from one to three climate improvement projects to be launched in the Washington School during the coming school year.
8. Organizing one task force to plan and implement each project identified, and assisting each task force in planning its work.
9. Coordinating the work of each task force.
10. Keeping the parents, faculty, and students informed of the progress of the work of the team and its task forces.

At the first SIMT meeting, the statement should be discussed and appropriate modifications made. It should then be accepted by the team members. The SIMT now is ready to develop a work plan. This is done

by assigning responsibility for each task outlined in the Statement of Purpose to one team member. That person then proceeds, with suggestions and assistance from others, to plan specific activities related to one task in the statement.

In order to carry out the tasks assigned in the Statement of Purpose, team members will need to learn a great deal about school climate. They should strive to become the school's in-house experts on factors and determinants of school climate, the research base for climate improvement, the rationale for climate improvement, and the change process. This handbook can serve as a basic text for acquiring some of this needed expertise. Additional resources also should be collected.

Each team meeting should be planned to stimulate the professional growth of the members. Once members acquire expertise in climate improvement, they can assume responsibility for planning and leading staff development for others.

The team, under the principal's leadership, manages the eight-step process. It is responsible for collecting baseline data; informing parents, staff, and students about the climate improvement concept; conducting the climate assessment; leading the planning/priority-setting workshop; and coordinating the work of the task forces. Initially, management teams typically meet bi-weekly. After the assessment has been completed, they usually can meet less frequently.

Step 2: Collect Baseline Data

Collection of baseline data is necessary so that the impact of the climate improvement project can be measured over time. The baseline data should be used to answer two questions: 1) To what extent does the school now have a positive or negative climate? and 2) To what extent are other symptoms of quality apparent in the school?

Data related to the first question may be obtained easily by using the CFK, Ltd., Profile, Part A (see Appendix B). This instrument has been validated to measure people's perceptions of the eight general climate factors described in Chapter 1. The instrument can be administered with confidence to staff members, parents who are knowledgeable about the school, and older students (grades 6 to 12).

Data related to the second question, concerning other symptoms of quality, may be obtained by using the problems checklist on page 8. Of course, if the climate is perceived as positive, respondents will tend to designate few such items as problems. Nevertheless, this checklist can provide useful baseline data.

Several management teams have gone beyond the problems check-list with more specific documentation readily available in school records. For example, attendance statistics, achievement data, and discipline referral records are kept routinely by most schools. Such records can be summarized easily for baseline data.

An early decision to be made by the management team is which baseline data to collect. Figure 3.2 lists six quality symptoms, which frequently are documented, as baseline data.

All six symptoms usually are sensitive to climate changes. However, the management team may choose not to collect data on one or two of the symptoms because of the difficulty of collecting the data or because a particular symptom will be unlikely to be affected significantly by climate improvement. For example, in a school in which pupil attendance already exceeds 96%, the team justifiably might choose not to collect attendance data.

Step 3: Raise the Awareness of Faculty, Students, and Parents

Students, parents, and staff must understand the rationale of the school climate concept and the steps involved in the process before the management team undertakes the assignment. The management team should plan a series of meetings to provide them with appropriate information. Two handouts for such meetings might include the definition of school climate and the list of climate symptoms and assumptions in Chapter 1.

The Association for Supervision and Curriculum Development (ASCD) distributes a kit consisting of three film strips with audio cassettes and related printed materials that can be used for orienting staff, parents, and students to the school climate concept (Howard 1980). Additional materials are available from CADRE, 1125 Moline St., Aurora, CO 80010; (303)361-6429.

Other activities include visiting schools that have implemented successful school climate projects, participation by faculty leaders on a school climate mini-audit visitation team (see page 26), and the establishment of a library of reference materials on school climate. Or it may be possible to invite a school climate expert or a leader from a school that has implemented a successful project to address your staff, student leaders, and parents. Specific recommendations regarding resource people and materials may be obtained from CADRE's national office.

By using the suggestions above, staff, students, and parents will become aware of the purposes and processes of school climate improve-

Figure 3.2
Quality Symptoms Affected Positively by Climate Improvements

Symptom	Assumption	How Measured
1. Achievement	1. As climate improves, pupils will learn more.	1.1 Longitudinal analyses of standardized test scores 1.2 Percentage of pupils earning high grades (A's and B's) 1.3 Percentage of pupils earning low grades (D's and F's) 1.4 Number and percentage of retentions in elementary schools
2. Attendance of Students and Staff	2. As climate improves, staff and student attendance will improve.	2.1 Total year attendance rates for staff and students 2.2 Attendance rates by comparable months (September of year 1 with September of Years 2 and 3) 2.3 Single period absences in secondary schools 2.4 Attendance at school-sponsored events (Parents' Night, key social, athletic, or cultural events)
3. Vandalism Costs	3. As climate improves, students will respect the school more and there will be less vandalism.	3.1 Head custodian's vandalism reports showing costs of damage done to the building by month and year (Costs should include value of staff time)
4. Dropout Rates (Secondary)	4. As climate improves, fewer pupils will drop out.	4.1 Annual dropout study and report
5. Discipline Problems	5. As climate improves, incidents of misbehavior will diminish.	5.1 Records of in-school and out-of-school suspensions 5.2 Records and analysis of the numbers of pupils referred to the office for disciplinary action. (Analysis should include number of individuals referred once, twice, three times) 5.3 Incidence of drug and alcohol abuse by secondary pupils 5.4 Fights on the playground (elementary), with monthly comparisons of Year 1 with the same months in Years 2 and 3. 5.5 Teacher questionnaire on perceptions of in-class discipline problems
6. Pupils Participation in School-sponsored Activities (Secondary)	6. As climate improves, more pupils will participate in school-sponsored activities	6.1 Survey all students in May to determine number of activities they have participated in during the year.

ment. They then will be ready for the next step, assessing a school's climate.

References

Fox, Robert S., et al. *School Climate Improvement: A Challenge to the School Administrator.* Bloomington, Ind.: Phi Delta Kappa, 1974.

Howard, Eugene R. *Improving School Climate: A Total Staff Development Kit.* Alexandria, Va.: Association for Supervision and Curriculum Development, 1980.

Chapter 4

Three Approaches to Assessing a School's Climate
STEP 4

This chapter presents three approaches to assessing a school's climate. Each is designed to provide information that can be used for climate improvement planning.

Approach 1: The CFK, Ltd., School Climate Profile

Part A of the CFK, Ltd., School Climate Profile (see Appendix B) provides information on the eight climate factors described in Chapter 1. Responses to Part A will answer the baseline data question: "To what extent is the climate of our school positive or negative?" and the parallel benchmark data question: "To what extent has the climate of our school improved?" Such benchmark data are essential for showing what impact the management team's interventions had on the climate of the school.

Parts B, C, and D of the profile provide information on people's perceptions of how well the 18 determinants of climate, described in Chapter 1, are operating in the school. An assessment of these 18 determinants is useful for answering the question: "What types of projects or activities should we plan in order to improve school climate?" Parts B, C, and D of the profile may be considered as diagnostic tools.

Data obtained from the CFK, Ltd., School Climate Profile will be much more powerful if gathered from people who see the school from different perspectives. Therefore, data should be gathered from teachers, students, administrators, support staff, and parents. Also, data based on people's perceptions of how things are or how they feel about them are important, because most behavior is motivated by the individual's perceptions of reality. Other kinds of information obtained from observation or behavior analysis also would be useful as part of a more extensive diagnostic effort.

The data provided by this profile may be analyzed in a number of ways:

1. Which climate factors or determinants are lowest on the scale? Which are highest? Perhaps the lowest ones should be considered as candidates for improvement projects.
2. For which climate factors or determinants are there large discrepancies between what is and what should be? If there is a large discrepancy, perhaps the reasons should be examined.
3. Are there marked discrepancies between how one group ranks a climate factor or determinant and how another group ranks it? If so, those discrepancies serve as a stimulus for further discussion and examination.

Approach 2: Mini-Audits

Mini-audits (see Appendix C) are adaptations of the CFK, Ltd., School Climate Profile developed by Eugene R. Howard and his colleagues in the Colorado Climate Improvement Project. These instruments, published by the Association for Supervision and Curriculum Development, are reprinted in Appendix C with permission from ASCD.

Mini-audits use the original climate determinants from the CFK, Ltd., Profile, but some have been combined to simplify the instrument. However, the individual items are very different from those of the CFK, Ltd., Profile. The items in the original profile are indicators that serve as goals for possible interventions, whereas the items in the ASCD instrument are descriptions of specific interventions to be considered.

Some of these interventions might be projects to strengthen existing programs and practices that are perceived as having a positive effect on school climate. Other interventions might be to initiate new practices, programs, or activities not currently operating. The activities, programs, and practices described in these instruments are those most often reported as being helpful in improving school climate.

Data from the mini-audits define strong and weak determinants, as do the CFK, Ltd., Profile data. However, the mini-audits also provide information regarding the extent to which various groups view certain interventions as promising. Thus the data will enable school leaders to launch projects that have substantial faculty, student, and parent support and to avoid projects perceived as having low potential for improving school climate.

Each section of the mini-audit is open-ended. Before administering the instruments, the management team may add items describing currently successful projects that, if strengthened, would affect the school's climate positively. The team also might wish to add new items that, in its view, have potential for improving school climate.

Management team members also may wish to edit some of the items in order to describe more precisely the interventions being considered. Items may be eliminated if they seem inappropriate for a particular school. However, items should not be dropped simply because the school is not implementing the idea. Dropping such items can deprive the management team of important information about the respondents' attitudes toward new ideas that may have high potential.

Respondents to the mini-audits may be staff members, informed students, and parents who are well acquainted with the school's programs and activities. It is not appropriate to ask people to respond who have little knowledge of the school.

There is some repetition of the mini-audit items. This occurs because some activities, projects, and programs will, if working well, have an impact on more than one climate determinant.

In administering the instrument, the management team may wish to organize the respondents into groups of three. Even though each member of the group would complete the instrument individually, the group leader could encourage discussion and sharing of information regarding the items as the group proceeds through the instrument together.

Approach 3: The Visitation Team Mini-Audit

One of the outcomes of the Colorado Climate Improvement Project (1979 to 1983) was an approach for assessing the climate of a school without using a printed instrument. Instead, information related to climate determinants is obtained through structured interviews by members of a visiting team.

This approach is fast and efficient. Assessment and priority-setting can be conducted in a day and a half. It avoids the use of questionnaires, which require hours to collate and to do statistical analyses of the data. It is, however, somewhat more costly because it requires the services of a trained consultant and involves staff from other schools.

The process consists of the following steps:

1. *Forming the Visiting Team.* The management team invites from one to four principals of nearby schools to provide the services of two or three of their most competent faculty members. These faculty members should be recognized leaders who have proficiency in interviewing, have good listening skills, and are likely to be receptive to the kinds of projects typically considered for climate improvement efforts. They need not have prior training in the eight-step process of climate improvement; they will learn a great deal about the concept and process in a very short time, thus benefiting themselves and their schools.

2. *Scheduling.* Interview schedules are arranged so that each visiting team member conducts five or six interviews during the one-day visit. Each teacher is scheduled individually for a 40- to 60-minute interview. Groups of other staff members (for example, secretaries, cooks, and custodians), groups of student leaders, and groups of parent leaders also are interviewed. A school with a faculty of 30 generally can be served by a visiting team of seven or eight persons.

3. *Awareness Materials for the Visiting Team.* Before the visit, team members are provided with awareness materials, including descriptions of the climate determinants and factors, an outline of the eight-step process, a paper describing interview techniques, and details regarding the visitation schedule.

4. *Training the Visiting Team.* A consultant provides the members of the visiting team with training on the climate concept, the rationale for the process and the assessment, and the interviewing techniques. This training session usually is scheduled for two hours during the evening before the visitation day.

5. *Conducting Interviews.* Visiting team members conduct the interviews using questions designed to identify current activities, practices and programs in the school that are having a positive impact on the school's climate. There is no attempt during the interviews to identify weaknesses or specific problems; this is done at another time. Rather, the mini-audit is designed to identify current practices in the school that could, if strengthened, have a positive impact on the school's climate.

6. *Compiling the Information.* Information obtained from all interviewers is compiled on forms designed for that purpose. This task usually is scheduled for 3:00 p.m. to 5:00 p.m. on the day of the visit.

7. *Producing the Report.* The following morning the information provided by the interviews is typed on report forms, and the first draft of the report is duplicated. This report then is used as the basis for the priority-setting workshop (see Chapter 5), which usually is scheduled for the afternoon of the second day.

8. *Planning and Further Training.* While the report is being typed and duplicated, the visiting team, the consultant, and the school management team are planning the priority-setting workshop and postworkshop activities. They also are receiving training in task force organization and management (see Chapter 6).

In a little more than a day and a half, the climate assessment is completed, a first draft of the report is produced, the priority-setting workshop is conducted, and follow-up activities are structured.

The focus on the positive aspects of a school is readily apparent in the assessment and priority-setting steps. Assessment is not intended to identify a school's problems; rather, it is designed to define a school's strengths and to answer the question: How can we do better what we already are doing well?

The visitation team mini-audit uses a nonthreatening, positive approach because a high level of trust is needed to facilitate information gathering. A problem audit, a somewhat different process, can be done later.

All three approaches to climate assessment presented in this chapter can be used for setting priorities, the subject of the next chapter.

Chapter 5

Organizing and Managing the Priority-Setting Workshop
STEP 5

Once the information from the climate assessment process is collected, it must be translated into decisions that will lead to improvement. This is done through a priority-setting workshop, the basic
purpose of which is to answer the question: "Which determinants
should we work on now?"

Ideally, the staff, parents, and students should undertake school improvement projects for all 18 climate determinants. But this is unrealis-
tic and no doubt would be overwhelming for the management team
to support 18 projects. Thus the workshop becomes the mechanism
for involving people in setting priorities as to which determinants to
work on.

Rationale for the Workshop

A negative school climate may be manifested by such *symptoms*
as discipline problems, absenteeism, alienation, or apathy. However,
focusing only on symptoms does not get at the root *causes* behind
the symptoms. These can be found only in the school's climate determinants. Therefore, it is important that the priority-setting workshop
focus on climate determinants, not on symptoms or problems.

Furthermore, the focus of the workshop should be on strengthening
those positive climate determinants already existing in the school. This

emphasis on the positive helps to create islands of excellence in the school, which in turn stimulates school pride and cohesiveness.

The outcome of the priority-setting workshop should be a series of activities, projects, or programs that positively affect the school's climate, and thereby have an impact on the symptoms.

Organization of the Workshop

The priority-setting workshop is designed to answer the following five questions:

1. Which of the climate improvement determinants included in the assessment have the greatest potential, if strengthened, for making a positive impact on the climate of the school?

2. For each determinant, what could a task force do to strengthen those activities, projects, and programs that already are having a positive effect on the school's climate?

3. For each determinant, what could a task force do to strengthen those activities, projects, and programs that could have a positive effect but are not yet functioning well?

4. Which task forces should be formed?

5. Who wants to work on these task forces?

Carrying out these objectives for the workshop involves eight steps:

1. *Structuring*. The workshop leader explains the purpose of the workshop and the procedures to be followed to accomplish the workshop's objectives.

2. *Reporting the Assessment Results*. A member of the management team summarizes the findings of the assessment and defines for the group each of the climate determinants to be considered.

3. *Initial Prioritization (optional)*. Using a Prioritization Preference Sheet (see Figure 5.1), which lists all the climate determinants, each workshop participant selects the three determinants that he or she feels would, if strengthened, have the greatest positive impact on improving the climate of the school.

4. *Brainstorming*. Workshop participants are organized in small groups. Each group considers one climate determinant by responding to the question: "If we were to form a task force to strengthen this climate determinant in our school, what might that task force do?" Each brainstorming group writes suggestions on large sheets of poster paper.

5. *Prioritizing*. Each brainstorming group is asked to choose the six to eight feasible ideas that the group feels have the greatest potential for strengthening climate.

Figure 5.1

Prioritization Preference Sheet
School Climate Determinants

Please circle the answers of the **three** determinants that, in your opinion, would affect the climate of the school most positively if they were strengthened.

Program Determinants:

    1. Active learning

    2. Individualized performance expectations/varied reward systems

    3. Varied learning environments and flexible curriculum and extracurricular activities

    4. Appropriate support and structure

    5. Rules cooperatively determined

Process Determinants:

    6. Problem solving, decision making, and resolving conflicts

    7. Improvement of school goals and planning for the future

    8. Effective communications

    9. Autonomy with accountability

    10. Effective teaching/learning strategies

Material Determinants:

    11. Adequate resources

    12. Supportive and efficient logistical systems

    13. Suitability of school plant

Note: *Determinants listed are from the ASCD Mini-Audit #1 and #2. Before reproducing this form, eliminate any determinants that have not been included in your assessment.*

6. *Reporting*. Each brainstorming group reports its six to eight recommendations to the entire workshop. Each large brainstorming sheet is then posted so that all ideas are visible.

7. *Final Prioritizing of Determinants*. Again using the Prioritization Preference Sheet, each workshop participant selects the three determinants that he or she feels would have the greatest positive impact on the climate of the school. The results of the voting are tallied, and the one to three determinants selected for strengthening are announced.

8. *Obtaining Volunteers*. The workshop leader or the principal describes how the task forces will function and asks for volunteers to serve on them. The time and places of the first task force meetings are then announced.

This workshop requires from three to four hours. It may be completed in a single half-day session or in two sessions on different days. If it is done in two sessions, the first might be devoted to assessment feedback and the second to brainstorming and prioritization. Somewhat more time may be needed for larger faculties because of the larger number of brainstorming groups reporting back.

All faculty members and instructional aides should participate in the workshop. Many schools also include informed parents and students. Try to assign one parent and one student to each brainstorming group. Also, some central office personnel may have considerable skill in conducting workshops. Invite these persons to serve in leadership roles.

The workshop leader is crucial to the success of the brainstorming and priority-setting process. Ideally, the leader should have strong group process skills. However, an inexperienced person can operate a successful workshop by carefully following the procedures outlined in this chapter. The workshop leader should be an individual who is highly respected by the faculty and who can keep the group on task. A common problem in workshop settings is keeping the activities on schedule. The leader must insist that established schedules be respected.

Running the Workshop

This section provides detailed instructions for the eight steps in running the priority-setting workshop.

Step 1: Structuring. In preparation for the workshop, the management team should:

- Prepare the agenda and have copies to give to each participant on arrival at the workshop.

- Choose a location for the workshop so that each brainstorming group of four to six persons will be able to work at a table without disturbing others. The school cafeteria or library is usually adequate for this purpose. For the session in which assessment results are shared, provide an overhead projector and screen and, for large groups, a sound system.
- Assist the individual who is responsible for presenting and interpreting the climate assessment results. Visuals and handouts must be ready before the workshop.
- Prepare enough copies of the Prioritization Preference Sheets so that each participant will have one for the preliminary prioritization activity (if included) and one for the final prioritization activity.
- Provide for each table at least two large sheets of poster paper for recording brainstorming ideas. Have extra sheets available. Also provide each table with two felt-tip pens, a roll of masking tape, copies of the Brainstorming and Prioritization Activity Instruction Sheets (see Appendix D), extra copies of the summary of the assessment findings, and a sign indicating which determinant is to be discussed.
- Assign one member of the management team to provide structure for each group. This person's role is to make sure that the instruction sheets and the rules for brainstorming (see Appendix D) are followed. Poorly structured brainstorming groups can deteriorate quickly into complaint sessions, long-winded debates, or the telling of war stories.
- Agree in advance of the workshop on the number of task forces to be formed (one, two, or three). This is important for Step 7 (Prioritizing) and Step 8 (Asking for Volunteers).
- Determine in advance of the workshop the number of brainstorming-prioritizing groups that will be needed. This number can be approximated by dividing the total number of participants by five, which is the ideal group size. If there are many participants, it may be necessary to have more than one brainstorming group for each topic.

At the opening session the workshop leader explains the purpose of the workshop and describes the procedures to be followed. The participants should know that they will be asked to use the assessment information as a basis for making judgments about the relative merits of several possible climate improvement activities.

Step 2: Reporting the Assessment Results. The assessment results are reported to workshop participants on summary forms (see Appendix B and Appendix C). A different format is used if the assessment is done by a visiting team. The summary forms can be presented as visuals on an overhead projector or they can be duplicated and distributed to workshop participants.

To assist in the interpretation of the assessment results, an interpretation sheet should be prepared for each climate determinant (see Appendix B and Appendix C). These interpretation sheets are distributed to each workshop participant.

In summarizing the information, the presenter proceeds sequentially through all of the visuals or handouts, defining each climate determinant (see Chapter 1 for definitions) and interpreting the information by referring to the interpretation sheet and by making such clarifying comments as may be appropriate.

Participants should be reminded periodically during the presentation that they will be asked to use this information as one basis for making some important judgments during the prioritizing portions of the workshop.

Step 3: Initial Prioritization. This step will be necessary only if your workshop group is very small. Brainstorming groups are most effective when they have from four to six members. If the number of participants in the workshop is too small to provide at least four members in each group, it is advisable to reduce the number of determinants with an initial prioritization. Under these circumstances, the Prioritization Preference Sheet should be modified to include only those determinants under consideration.

The workshop leader distributes one prioritization sheet to each participant. The participants make their choices, and the results are tabulated at once. Then the climate determinants to be discussed in the brainstorming session are announced, and a sign giving the name of the determinants is placed on each table.

The participants may take a short break while the prioritization results are being tallied. But before they leave, they should be told that when they return, they are to choose the determinant they wish to discuss by sitting at the table with the sign of their choice. There is only one rule: each group may have no more than six members. If six persons already are seated at a table, then the participant must make a second choice.

Step 4: Brainstorming. Once the participants have selected their tables, the workshop leader reiterates the purpose of the brainstorming activity and describes the facilitator's role. The leader emphasizes the importance of following the procedures on the instruction sheet and summarizes the rules for brainstorming (see Appendix D). The leader asks each group to select a recorder; then the brainstorming session begins.

While the brainstorming is in progress, the workshop leader moves from group to group responding to questions, making procedural suggestions, and observing the progress of the groups. Occasionally groups have to be reminded that their role is to make suggestions for activities, projects, and programs to be implemented by task forces, not to make detailed prescriptions of what all teachers should do. Such prescriptions, if appropriate, come later during the prioritizing stage. Sometimes groups also tend to suggest things for the school board, parents, or the school administration to do. Again, remind the brainstorming group that their charge is to develop ideas potentially useful to a task force.

While moving from group to group, the workshop leader should encourage participants to get as many ideas on paper as quickly as possible. There is a tendency for groups to want to discuss each item as it is presented. Facilitators and the workshop leader should discourage this practice because it stifles spontaneity and bogs down the process. Remind the groups that there will be time for discussion during the prioritizing stage.

After approximately 40 minutes of brainstorming, most groups are running out of new ideas. At this time the leader directs the groups to begin the prioritizing process.

Step 5: Prioritizing. In this step the groups begin discussing and evaluating the feasibility and probable impact of the activities, projects, and programs that have been identified in the brainstorming session. They are asked to respond to the question: Which of the ideas suggested would, if implemented, have the most positive impact on the climate of our school? They then recommend six to eight ideas to be considered by a climate improvement task force.

As priority items are agreed on by each group, the recorder makes a star in front of the items listed on the brainstorming sheets. Some groups will combine similar suggestions under a single heading. During the prioritizing process a number of items will be eliminated because they will be judged impractical because of limited resources or lack of commitment. Agreement generally is reached by consensus.

As soon as all groups have finished the prioritizing task, the leader calls for individual group reports.

Step 6: Reporting. Before reports begin, the workshop leader should set a time limit for each report, typically three minutes. If such a time limit is not enforced, this portion of the workshop can become excessively long and boring. The group facilitator gives the report, and the recorder assists by holding up the brainstorming sheet as it is being described.

After giving the report, the facilitator posts the brainstorming sheets on the wall with masking tape so all reports can be seen by all participants. After the workshop, the school secretary should type the ideas from the brainstorming sheets and highlight the priority ones, so they will be available for the task forces. No idea generated in the workshop should be lost; some of them will be appropriate for more than one climate determinant.

Step 7: Prioritizing the Determinants. After all reports have been presented, the participants complete their Prioritization Preference Sheet and the results are tallied. While the tallying is in progress, the workshop leader or the principal summarizes the major recommendations made by the brainstorming groups and explains that the task forces to be formed will use these ideas as a point of departure for planning.

Prior to the workshop, the management team should agree on the number of task forces to be formed. The participants are now ready to form task forces.

Step 8: Obtaining Task Force Volunteers. Each participant receives an index card and indicates on it which task force he or she would like to join. Participation on a task force should be voluntary since it involves a considerable time investment and many teachers already may be committed fully to other school improvement activities. All participants in the workshop are eligible to join a task force — parents, students, and support staff.

Once the cards have been collected and the task force groups are formed, there is a brief meeting to determine the time and place of each task force's first meeting. With appropriate concluding remarks by the workshop leader, the workshop is then adjourned.

The brainstorming-prioritizing workshop is a key activity in the overall climate improvement process. If it has been well planned and efficiently managed, it will contribute substantially to the cohesiveness of the school. By focusing on climate determinants rather than specific problems, the workshop participants deal with the existing characteristics of the school and thus are better prepared to investigate some of the *causes* of a poor school climate.

The management team may now proceed with confidence with the organization of task forces, which can develop plans to improve the school using specific suggestions that generally are viewed as promising.

Chapter 6

Task Forces Go to Work
STEPS 6 AND 7

With the priorities for school climate improvement identified, the task forces begin to plan and then undertake specific projects to improve the school's climate. This chapter will deal with how the task forces are organized, how they plan and manage their work, and how they evaluate their own effectiveness.

Role of the Task Force

A task force is a planning, working, and learning group — not a studying and recommending group. It is an action group; it does not think up things for others to do. It has accepted responsibility for planning and implementing school improvement activities.

Short-term task forces may address specific problems, solve those problems, and then disband. However, task forces usually are long-term operations — from two to four years — because of the complex nature of their tasks. The membership and objectives may change from year to year, but the overall focus remains constant.

Task forces are delegated authority to carry out those activities specified in the management team's charge statement (see Figure 6.1). In a schoolwide climate improvement project, one task force is set up for each determinant identified in the priority-setting workshop. Some task forces may be sponsored by the parents' association or by the student council. Most, however, are sponsored by the faculty.

Figure 6.1

Sample Charge Statement to a New Task Force

The _____ Task Force is charged with accomplishing the following:

1. To study the recommendations made by the groups in the priority-setting workshop and to develop objectives and activities consistent with those recommendations.
2. To study and discuss other promising approaches for positively influencing the determinants and to develop objectives and activities consistent with those approaches.
3. To agree on an overall improvement plan for the determinant.
4. To seek approval of the improvement plan from the management team.
5. Following approval, to implement the plan by giving specific task assignments and setting target dates.
6. To foster professional growth among all task force members so that the group's impact on climate will be enhanced.
7. To report the task force's progress to the management team, the faculty, parents, students, the superintendent's office, and the board of education.
8. To recruit new talent to the task force if needed to achieve new objectives.
9. To replace non-functioning members of the task force if necessary.
10. To evaluate the task force's work in terms of its objectives and to report this information to the management team and to other interested parties.
11. To evaluate the effectiveness of the processes used by the task force in decision making, problem solving, planning, and managing its work and to modify its procedures in accordance with such evaluations.
12. To evaluate periodically the effectiveness of each of the task force's school improvement projects so that each project can be improved at each stage of its development.

Task Force Organization and Management

Members of the task force may be faculty, support staff, students, parents, or community leaders — anyone with talent and skills to contribute to the project and who is willing to work. The original task force should be small — four to six members. Later, as the task force takes on new duties, the membership may be expanded.

The task force leader is the key person in determining the task force's effectiveness. The leader must be a good planner and expediter. Much of the expediting is done between meetings prior to the time that specific activities are planned and implemented. See Figure 6.2 for a sample job description for a task force leader.

Figure 6.2

Sample Job Description of Task Force Leader

1. To facilitate the task force's planning so that specific action plans are developed.
2. To serve as the task force's representative on the management team.
3. To present the original action plan to the management team for approval and to present changes to the plan when proposed.
4. To provide periodic progress reports to the management team and others on the task force's accomplishments.
5. To expedite implementation of the action plan by encouraging task force members to complete their assigned duties; also to monitor the timeline so that planned activities occur on schedule.
6. To encourage professional growth of task force members by recommending appropriate readings and discussing ideas related to climate improvement and by arranging visits to other schools where similar projects are under way.
7. To encourage the expansion of the task force's action plan as members become more skillful in distinguishing between less significant and more significant improvement projects.
8. To be responsible to the management team and the principal for the effectiveness of the task force's work.

An effective task force has an established meeting time and place. Calendars should be checked to avoid schedule conflicts so that the meetings are well attended. A member who must be absent should contact the leader and provide a progress report if one is scheduled. Also, absent members should contact the leader after the meeting for a brief report of what happened. Most task forces meet monthly. A sample agenda for a task force meeting is shown in Figure 6.3.

It is essential that each task force plan its work with each task force member assigned a clearly defined responsibility. There should be no free rides. The work plan should be flexible. As tasks are accomplished, they are eliminated from the plan and new tasks are added as a result of the group's ongoing planning activity. A planning sheet should be prepared for each task force objective. See Figure 6.4 on page 42 for a sample planning sheet.

```
┌─────────────────────────────────────────────────────────────────────┐
│                             Figure 6.3                                │
│                                                                       │
│                  Sample Task Force Meeting Agenda                     │
│                                                                       │
│   3:00 to 3:30 Professional Growth Time                               │
│                 • Discussion of books, articles, research reports     │
│                 • Discuss visits to other schools                     │
│                 • Hear presentation by an outside expert              │
│                 • Discussion of possible growth activities for the    │
│                   total faculty or other task forces                  │
│   3:30 to 4:00 Progress Reports                                       │
│                 • Each member reports on activities related to the    │
│                   action plan                                         │
│   4:00 to 4:20 Suggestions for New Activities to be Added to Action   │
│                Plan                                                    │
│   4:20 to 4:30 Formative Evaluation                                   │
│                 • Evaluation of effectiveness of activities completed │
│                 • Process observer's report on group's effectiveness  │
└─────────────────────────────────────────────────────────────────────┘
```

A portion of each meeting should be devoted to professional growth activities. In fact, the work of the task force itself might well be the basic vehicle for professional growth as well as for school improvement.

As a task force carries out its work, it may be necessary to add subgroups. For example, a task force charged with improving communications may begin with a set of activities related to school-home communications. Later a sub-group may be formed to deal with improving communications among student cliques and another to deal with improving student-teacher communications. With the addition of subgroups, the task force might invite new members whose talents would contribute to the new objectives.

If possible, each task force should have a small budget to cover such items as travel costs for visits to other schools, a small collection of professional materials related to the task force's objectives, and other materials needed to carry out its work. Some schools have established a "School Improvement" line item in the existing budget to cover such costs.

Task Force Evaluation

Ideally, each task force should undertake three kinds of evaluation:

1. Evaluation of the task force's impact in carrying out its objectives;
2. Evaluation of the processes the task force has used in making decisions, solving problems, developing its plans, and managing its work; and

3. Formative evaluation designed to improve the effectiveness of the task force's projects at each stage of their development.

Most task forces will require assistance from an outside consultant in order to design their evaluation procedures. Such assistance may be available from the school district central office or from a nearby university.

Evaluating the impact of the task force's work requires more formal procedures involving collection and analysis of data. Process and formative evaluation is primarily for the task force's own use, to help it

---

Figure 6.4

Sample Task Force Plan of Work

Objective: Improve communications between teachers and pupils and provide each pupil with faculty support in personal problem solving and decision making.

Responsibility: Jim Hanson

Assisted by: Marie Davis, Jo Ann Brown, Bill Buckner, Harold Jensen

Activities	Target Date	Responsibility
1. Provide task force members with information regarding successful programs	ongoing	Jim
2. Organize visits to other schools	Sept. 20 Oct. 15 Nov. 15	Bill
3. Design pilot project for Jefferson High School	Dec. 1	Harold and total task force
4. Design evaluation plan for pilot project	Dec. 1	Jo Ann
5. Plan and conduct inservice sessions for pilot project advisors	Oct. 15 Nov. 15 Dec. 5 and ongoing	Marie
6. Keep faculty, parents, and students informed of projects	ongoing	Jim and Marie

improve its own effectiveness. Some task forces have found it helpful to use a process observer whose responsibility is to make suggestions for improving the task force's effectiveness. Figure 6.5 is a checklist a process observer can use for observing how task force members work together as a group.

Figure 6.5

Process Observer Checklist

This checklist can be used by the process observer to record the group interaction during a task force meeting. It is recommended that the last 10 minutes of each meeting be reserved for the process observer to lead a discussion on ways the task force can improve its own effectiveness.

1. To what extent were participants involved in the meeting?
   * Were there any who did not participate?
   * Did a few dominate the discussion?

2. To what extent were the following kinds of behavior observed?
   * Information sharing
   * Supporting comments
   * Reflecting
   * Interpreting
   * Comments seeking further information or clarification
   * Sharing of feelings or emotions
   * Group facilitating comments
   * Blocking maneuvers
   * Speech making for ego satisfaction

3. To what extent did the task force leader structure the meeting and facilitate the agenda?
4. To what extent were the communication lines one way between the leader and the participants as opposed to participants communicating with each other?
5. Did the discussion stick to the subject? Was it necessary for the leader to pull the group back to discussing the subject?
6. Were any decisions made? If so, what decision-making process was used?
7. Does any one individual dominate the group?
8. Does the group exhibit active listening by focusing on what is said?

This checklist was developed by Eugene R. Howard of the Colorado Department of Education for use by the Colorado League of Schools for Climate Improvement.

Task forces are the organizational structure that makes change manageable and climate improvement achievable. They provide a structure for staff, student, and community involvement in the complex task of making a school accommodate human needs. The task forces develop pride, ownership, and cohesiveness in a school. Mary Lou Zarlengo, the principal quoted at the beginning of Chapter 1, has nine task forces working on school improvement in her school, which involve every teacher and dozens of parents. Their work is coordinated by a management team of parents and staff. Comments Ms. Zarlengo:

> A school organized for systematic change is very different from a school organized for maintaining the status quo. It looks different; it functions differently; it feels different.

Chapter 7
Evaluating the Impact of School Climate Improvement
STEP 8

This chapter shows how the impact of the school's climate improvement efforts can be measured and reported, using examples from three school climate projects. Impact is measured in terms of what happens, over time, to the climate symptoms selected for documentation with baseline data (Step 2). Impact is reported in terms of the underlying assumptions defined when baseline data were collected. For example, if in a given project the assumption is that as climate improves pupils will learn more, then two questions related to this assumption for measuring impact might be: 1) Did the climate of our school improve over time? and 2) Are students learning more?

The extent to which climate is improved can be documented by using the CFK, Ltd., Profile, Part A. The extent to which students are learning more can be documented through a longitudinal analysis of test scores, through an analysis of the percentage of students earning high grades (As and Bs), or through a decline in the percentage of retentions.

Kiyo Yamata, an elementary principal in Colorado Springs, did a longitudinal study using the Iowa Test of Basic Skills reading scores over a five-year period to document the impact of his climate improvement project. Longitudinal studies in schools with substantial turnover of students is difficult, but not impossible, if one uses the scores only of pupils who have been enrolled in the school for two or more years.

In reporting the impact of climate improvement on learning, some schools disaggregated their data to show achievement trends for pupils from low-income families as compared to pupils from higher-income families. Thomas Currie, principal of a K-7 elementary school serving a low-income area in rural West Virginia, prepared his climate report by showing baseline data, the interventions used, and the outcomes achieved, but also by disaggregating the student achievement data in reading by low-income and higher-income families.

Using the disaggregated data, Currie was able to show that in 1981-82, 10% of the low-income third-graders scored in the lowest quartile. By 1983-84 none of these former third-graders was in the lowest quartile. Similar gains were documented in the sixth-graders' scores. Also, the percentage of low-income pupils declined in the second quartile and increased in the top two quartiles. During the same period, the percentage of higher-income pupils in the top two quartiles also increased. Thus the gains made by low-income pupils apparently were not made at the expense of those from higher-income families.

In his impact report Currie describes 27 interventions that he believes contributed to the overall improvement of the school's quality. Some interventions used findings from effective schools research; others reflected climate improvement efforts. Some examples of interventions used were:

- Assessing student progress every three weeks and reporting to parents.
- Enforcing promotion and retention policy.
- Using the Assertive Discipline code with parent notifications.
- Increasing attendance monitoring and parent notifications.
- Eliminating ability grouping.
- Forming a school climate improvement team.
- Using peer observations.
- Improving staff evaluations.

Using baseline data, Currie was able to document the following improvements in his climate impact report:

- Pupil attendance increased from 90% to 93%.
- Discipline referrals declined from 553 to 187 in one year.
- Vandalism stopped.
- Teacher attendance increased from 96% to 97.1%.
- Internal and external suspensions increased initially but then declined.

The Pennsylvania Climate Improvement Project, a pilot project in two schools sponsored by the Pennsylvania Department of Education and the Pennsylvania Commission on Crime and Delinquency, documented improvement in climate factors and determinants by using the CFK, Ltd., Profile, Parts A, B, C, and D, and improvements in conditions supportive of teaching by using the Pennsylvania Educational Quality Assessment. Symptoms of quality documented from school records included:

- Dropout rate for School Two decreased by 19%; School One had no dropouts in either year of the study.
- Suspensions in School One decreased by 37%; in School Two by 17%.
- Class cutting was reduced by 53% in School One and almost 100% in School Two.
- Attendance of both students and staff improved in both schools.
- Delinquency figures showed a reduction in offenses and fewer arrests, thus confirming an initial assumption that there is a relationship between school climate and delinquent behavior outside the school. The number of repeat offenders was reduced by 44%.

Interventions included expansion of active learning; expansion of the rewards system; increased student, parent, and staff involvement in decision making, planning, and school improvement projects; improvements in the physical environment in School One; an in-school suspension program; and higher academic standards.

The three examples of climate impact studies described above represent *correlational* evaluation. One cannot claim that a more positive climate *caused* gains in achievement or improved attendance or reduction in suspensions. Causality can be determined only if variables are carefully controlled. That is too complex and costly a process for most schools to undertake.

Nevertheless, correlational data can be convincing if the assumptions underlying the project interventions have been made clear from the beginning. By stating these assumptions and by collecting ample baseline data, those responsible for carrying out the school climate study will be in a much better position to assess the impact of the interventions and to document the outcomes.

Chapter 8
Why Do It?

One of the authors (Howard) recently met a teacher from a junior high school where he had served as a consultant. Three years ago this school had completed its assessment and initiated three climate improvement task forces.

"How is the climate in your school now?" he asked.

"It's godawful," the teacher responded. "Most of us just go into our classrooms, close the door, teach our classes, and go home at three o'clock."

"I'm sorry to hear that," he said, "but what happened to the plans your task forces made? What happened to your climate improvement project?"

"Well," she said, "The task forces did some good work for a while, then our principal was transferred. Our new principal didn't support the project. I guess he had ideas of his own."

For a consultant who, only three years ago, had spent a lot of time and effort on this school's improvement project, hearing this bad news was disheartening. But it illustrates how critical the role of the principal is for maintaining the momentum of a climate project. The good news, however, is that this does not usually happen. In schools that follow the eight-step process, positive results consistently occur. The unsuccessful projects have typically occurred in schools with weak or unstable leadership, or where task forces were not provided with adequate support or encouragement.

48

What are some of the characteristics of those schools that have launched successful projects?

1. They are cohesive places. People know what their school stands for. In such schools the people communicate with one another, respect one another, and work with one another for school improvement.

2. They are caring places. People in such schools care about one another and the school as an institution. People feel a sense of pride and ownership that comes from their having a role in making the school a better place.

3. They are places that serve human needs. Procedures, rules, regulations, and policies serve the people in the schools.

Following are some examples of what happens in schools that have done climate studies:

An elementary principal reports that the percentage of pupils achieving in the lowest quartile in reading has declined by almost 100% over three years. The same principal reports that discipline referrals to the office decreased from 553 to 187 in one year.

A custodian tells a principal, "In other schools where I have worked the cafeteria was always a mess after lunch hour. Here the children clean up after themselves. Why is that?"

A principal calls the consultant and says, "We now have over half of our teachers working on school improvement task forces. Morale has never been higher. I've never worked with a faculty with such a positive attitude."

A state department official reports that his state's pilot projects, funded from delinquency prevention grants, have resulted in higher achievement, fewer discipline problems, and a lowered delinquency rate. For the first time there is data that suggest that a positive school climate affects the attitudes and behavior of youth in the community as well as in the school.

A superintendent of a large district in a Western state reports that his districtwide climate project has been recognized as exemplary by the state superintendent of public instruction. The superintendent and his staff are now helping other school districts design climate improvement projects. "We are proving," he says, "that pupils learn more in schools with positive climates."

A high school principal reports a sharply reduced failure rate, an increase in the percentage of honor students, and a reduced dropout rate. "These things happened," he says, "because our school's climate improved."

A California high school that had lost its accreditation because of the poor quality of its programs initiated a climate improvement project. Three years later the school was recognized by the state for its high achievement.

The examples above and several other case studies are documented in *School Climate Improvement: Leadership and Process* (1986) by Eugene R. Howard, published by CADRE Publications Center, 1125 Moline St., Aurora, CO 80010.

We now have had enough experience with climate improvement to believe that nothing of substance improves until the school's climate does. How people feel about their school can either facilitate or sabotage change. School improvement is fueled by people's emotions. As the climate of the school becomes more positive, discipline problems, vandalism, and violence subside; attendance and achievement improve; the number of dropouts declines; people smile more, are more respectful and helpful to others, and assume more responsibility for the well-being of the school. This is why we do it.

Appendices

The Appendices include all the instruments for conducting school climate studies referred to in this text. A brief description of each instrument is provided below.

All of these instruments are copyrighted, but any purchaser of this book may reproduce them for use in school climate studies or for other purposes. Written permission is not required. However, they are not to be reproduced for resale to others.

Appendix A, Rate Your School's Climate, is a short version of the CFK, Ltd., School Climate Profile. It can be used to familiarize a school staff with the components of school climate or for graduate students in a seminar on school evaluation or school improvement. It provides only a rough measure of school climate and is not intended as a substitute for the complete CFK, Ltd., School Climate Profile.

Appendix B is the complete CFK, Ltd., School Climate Profile, which has been used widely in school climate studies for several years. It provides an assessment of people's perceptions of what are and what should be the positive climate factors and determinants in a school, and thus helps a school staff decide what should be the priorities for improvement projects. It also serves as a benchmark against which a school can measure climate change. It takes from 20 to 25 minutes to administer the instrument.

Data generated from this instrument will be more valid if collected from those who view the school from different perspectives. Thus

51

teachers, administrators, support staff, students, and parents should be invited to fill out the instrument.

Analysis of the data from this instrument can identify positive and negative climate factors, discrepancies in climate factors between what is and what should be, and discrepancies in perceptions among the various groups filling out the instrument. Such analyses can be used for determining what improvement projects should be undertaken and for investigating reasons for the discrepancies.

Appendix C includes Mini-Audits 1 and 2. They were developed by Eugene Howard and were originally published in 1980 by the Association for Supervision and Curriculum Development. Although based on the CFK, Ltd., School Climate Profile, these two mini-audits are different in that they were designed to assess school climate in terms of specific activities, programs, or practices that have been identified as being helpful in improving school climate. These instruments may be modified by adding activities, programs, or practices unique to a particular school. Mini-Audit 1 deals with activities and projects that affect school climate positively. Mini-Audit 2 deals with the process and material determinants of school climate.

Appendix D is the Brainstorming and Prioritizing Activity Instruction Sheet. It includes the rules for brainstorming and instructions for the group leader in carrying out the prioritizing activity. It was originally published in *School Climate Improvement: A Staff Development Kit* distributed by the Association for Supervision and Curriculum Development. Copyright © 1980 by ASCD. Reprinted with permission.

Rate Your School's Climate

School Climate Factors

To what extent is this factor a strength or weakness of your school?	Very Strong	Somewhat Strong	Somewhat Weak	Very Weak
Respect				
Trust				
High Morale				
Opportunities for Input				
Continuous Academic and Social Growth				
Cohesiveness				
School Renewal				
Caring				

School Climate Determinants

To what extent is this determinant a strength or weakness of your school?	Very Strong	Somewhat Strong	Somewhat Weak	Very Weak
Program Determinants				
Opportunities for Active Learning				
Individualized Performance Expectations				

Varied Learning Environments				
Flexible Curriculum and Extracurricular Activities				
Support and Structure Appropriate to Learner's Maturity				
Rules Cooperatively Determined				
Varied Reward Systems				
Process Determinants				
Problem-Solving Ability				
Improvement of School Goals				
Identifying and Working with Conflicts				
Effective Communications				
Involvement in Decision Making				
Autonomy with Accountability				
Effective Teaching-Learning Strategies				
Ability to Plan for the Future				
Material Determinants				
Adequate Resources				
Supportive and Efficient Logistical System				
Suitability of School Plant				

Appendix B
The CFK, Ltd., School Climate Profile

Purpose

This instrument gives you an opportunity to express your feelings about many aspects of your school's climate. Although it may not include every item you consider important in your school, it does provide an overall assessment of a school's climate. The instrument has four parts, covering 26 climate categories with five items for each category. The ratings for the various items in Parts A, B, C, and D of this instrument will help in deciding which climate factors should be looked at more intensively when engaging in school improvement projects.

Directions

1. Check the category you fall under:

   ____ Teacher   ____ Parent

   ____ Other professional staff   ____ Administrator in

   ____ Secretary, custodian, or   this school
   other support staff   ____ Administrator in

   ____ Student   central office

2. Read each item thoughtfully and indicate a rating under both the "What Is" column and the "What Should Be" column. Use the following scale to indicate your rating for each item in both columns:

   1 — Almost Never
   2 — Occasionally
   3 — Frequently
   4 — Almost Always

3. In the box at the bottom of each of the 26 sections, total your score. Your lowest possible score for each section would be 5; the highest 20.

Part A
General Climate Factors

	What Is:	What Should Be:
Respect:		
1. In this school even low achieving students are respected.		
2. Teachers treat students as persons.		
3. Parents are considered by this school as important collaborators.		
4. Teachers from one subject area or grade level respect those from other subject areas.		
5. Teachers in this school are proud to be teachers.		
Total		
Trust:		
1. Students feel that teachers are "on their side."		
2. While we don't always agree, we can share our concerns with each other openly.		
3. Our principal is a good spokesperson for our interests and needs before the superintendent and the board.		
4. Students can count on teachers to listen to their side of the story and to be fair.		
5. Teachers trust students to use good judgment.		
Total		
High Morale:		
1. This school makes students enthusiastic about learning.		

2. Teachers feel pride in this school and in its students.

3. Attendance is good; students stay away only for urgent and good reasons.

4. Parents, teachers, and students would rise to the defense of this school's program if it were challenged.

5. I like working in this school.

Total

Opportunity for Input:

1. I feel that my ideas are listened to and used in this school.

2. When important decisions are made about the programs in this school, I, personally, have heard about the plan beforehand and have been involved in some of the discussions.

3. Important decisions are made in this school by a governing council with representation from students, faculty, and administration.

4. While I obviously can't have a vote on every decision that is made in this school that affects me, I do feel that I can have some important input into that decision.

5. When all is said and done, I feel that I count in this school.

Total

Continuous Academic and Social Growth:

1. The teachers are "alive"; they are interested in life around them; they are doing interesting things outside of school.

2. Teachers in this school are "out in front," seeking better ways of teaching and learning.

3. Students feel that the school program is meaningful and relevant to their present and future needs.

4. The principal is growing and learning, too. He or she is seeking new ideas.

5. The school supports parent growth. Regular opportunities are provided for parents to be involved in learning activities and in examining new ideas.

Total

Cohesiveness:

1. Students would rather attend this school than transfer to another.

2. There is a "we" spirit in this school.

3. Administration and teachers collaborate toward making the school run effectively; there is little administrator-teacher tension.

4. Differences between individuals and groups (both faculty and students) are considered to contribute to the richness of the school, not as divisive influences.

5. New students and faculty members are made to feel welcome and part of the group.

Total

School Renewal:

1. When a problem comes up, this school has procedures for working on it; problems are seen as normal challenges, not as "rocking the boat."

2. Teachers are encouraged to innovate in their classroom rather than to conform.

3. When a student comes along who has special problems, this school works out a plan that helps that student.		
4. Students are encouraged to be creative rather than to conform.		
5. Careful effort is made, when new programs are introduced, to adapt them to the particular needs of this community and this school.		
Total	☐	☐

Caring:

1. There is someone in this school that I can always count on.		
2. The principal really cares about students.		
3. I think people in this school care about me as a person and are concerned about more than just how well I perform my role at school.		
4. I feel wanted and needed in this school.		
5. Most people at this school are kind.		
Total	☐	☐

Part B
Program Determinants

	What Is:	What Should Be:
Active Learning:		
1. Required textbooks and curriculum guides support rather than limit creative teaching and learning in our school.		
2. Students help to decide learning objectives.		

3. Opportunities are provided under school guidance to do something with what is learned.		
4. Teachers are actively learning, too.		
5. This school's program stimulates creative thought and expression.		
Total	☐	☐

Individualized Performance Expectations:

1. Each student's special abilities (intellectual, artistic, social, or manual) are challenged.		
2. Teachers use a wide range of teaching materials and media.		
3. The same homework assignment is not given to all students in the class.		
4. All students are not held to the same standards.		
5. Teachers know students as individuals.		
Total	☐	☐

Varied Learning Environments:

1. Many opportunities are provided for learning in individual and small-group settings, as well as in total classroom groups.		
2. Students have an opportunity to choose associations with teachers whose teaching styles are supportive of students' learning styles.		
3. Teachers use a wide range of teaching materials and media.		
4. The school program extends to settings beyond the school building for most students.		

5. Teachers and administrators have planned individualized inservice education programs to support their own growth.		
Total	☐	☐

Flexible Curriculum and Extracurricular Activities:

1. The school's program is appropriate for ethnic and minority groups.		
2. Teachers experiment with innovative programs.		
3. Students are given alternative ways of meeting curriculum requirements.		
4. Teachers are known to modify their lesson plans on the basis of student suggestions.		
5. Extracurricular activities appeal to each of the various subgroups of students.		
Total	☐	☐

Support and Structure Appropriate to Learners' Maturity:

1. The school's program encourages students to develop self-discipline and initiative.		
2. The needs of a few students for close supervision and high structure are met without making those students feel "put down."		
3. The administration is supportive of students.		
4. The administration is supportive of teachers.		
5. Faculty and staff want to help every student learn.		
Total	☐	☐

Rules Cooperatively Determined:

1. The school operates under a set of rules that were worked out with students, teachers, parents, and administration all participating.
2. Rules are few and simple.
3. Teachers and their students together work out rules governing behavior in the classroom.
4. Discipline (punishment) when given is fair and related to violations of agreed-on rules.
5. Most students and staff members obey the school's rules.

Total

Varied Reward Systems:

1. The grading system rewards students for their effort as related to their ability.
2. Students know the criteria used to evaluate their progress.
3. Teachers are rewarded for exceptionally good teaching.
4. The principal is aware of and lets staff and students know when they have done something particularly well.
5. Most students get positive feedback from faculty and staff.

Total

Part C
Process Determinants

	What Is:	What Should Be:
Problem-Solving Ability:		
1. Problems in this school are recognized and worked on openly and are not allowed to slide.		

2. If I have a school-related problem, I feel there are channels open to me to get the problem worked on.		
3. People in this school do a good job of examining a lot of alternative solutions first, before deciding to try one.		
4. Ideas from various ethnic and minority groups are sought in problem-solving efforts.		
5. People in this school solve problems; they don't just talk about them.		
Total		

Improvement of School Goals:

1. This school has set some goals as a school for this year and I know about them.		
2. I have set some personal goals for this year related to school, and I have shared these goals with someone else.		
3. Community involvement is sought in developing the school's goals.		
4. The goals of this school are used to provide direction for programs.		
5. The goals of this school are reviewed and updated.		
Total		

Identifying and Working with Conflicts:

1. In this school people with ideas or values different from the commonly accepted ones get a chance to be heard.		
2. There are procedures open to me for going to a higher authority if a decision has been made that seems unfair.		
3. This school believes there may be several alternative solutions to most problems.		

4. In this school the principal tries to deal with conflict constructively, not just "keep the lid on."		
5. When we have conflicts in this school, their resolution is constructive, not destructive.		
Total	☐	☐

Effective Communications:

1. Teachers feel free to communicate with the principal.		
2. I feel the teachers are friendly and easy to talk to.		
3. The principal talks with us frankly and openly.		
4. Teachers are available to students who want help.		
5. There is communication in our school between different groups — older teachers and younger ones, well-to-do students and poorer ones, black parents and white parents, etc.		
Total	☐	☐

Involvement in Decision Making:

1. Teachers help in selection of new staff members.		
2. Parents help to decide about new school programs.		
3. Decisions that affect this school are made by the superintendent and the central staff only after opportunity has been provided for discussion and input from the school's principal, staff, and students.		
4. I have influence on the decisions within the school that directly affect me.		

5. The student government makes important decisions.		
Total	☐	☐

Autonomy with Accountability:

1. Teachers, students, and parents help to evaluate this school's program.		
2. Teacher evaluation is used in improving teacher performance.		
3. Teachers or students can arrange to deviate from the prescribed program of the school.		
4. The principal encourages experimentation in teaching.		
5. Teachers are held accountable in this school for providing learning opportunities for each of their students.		
Total	☐	☐

Effective Teaching-Learning Strategies:

1. The teachers in this school know how to teach as well as what to teach.		
2. When one teaching strategy does not seem to be working for a particular student, the teacher tries another and does not blame the student for the initial failure.		
3. This community supports new and innovative teaching techniques.		
4. Inservice education programs available to teachers in this building help them keep up-to-date on the best teaching strategies.		
5. The school systematically encourages students to help other students with their learning activities.		
Total	☐	☐

Ability to Plan for the Future:		
1. In this school we keep "looking ahead"; we don't spend all our time "putting out fires."		
2. Our principal is an "idea" person.		
3. Parents and community leaders have opportunities to work with school officials at least once a year on "things we'd like to see happening in our school."		
4. Some of the programs in our school are termed "experimental."		
5. Our school is ahead of the times.		
Total		

Part D
Material Determinants

	What Is:	What Should Be:
Adequate Resources:		
1. There is sufficient staff in this school to meet the needs of its students.		
2. The instructional materials are adequate for our school program.		
3. Curriculum materials used in this school give appropriate emphasis and accurate facts regarding ethnic and minority groups and sex roles.		
4. Resources are provided so that students can take advantage of learning opportunities in the community through field trips, work-study arrangements, etc.		

5. Current teacher salaries in this community give fair recognition of the level of professional service rendered by teachers to the community.		
Total		

Supportive and Efficient Logistical System:

1. Teachers and students are able to get the instructional materials they need at the time they are needed.

2. This school provides opportunities for teachers to recommend and make judgments about priorities for resources needed in their program at budget time.

3. The support system of this school fosters creative and effective teaching/learning opportunities rather than hinders them.

4. Necessary materials and supplies for learning experiences are readily available as needed.

5. Simple non-time-consuming procedures exist for the acquisition and use of resources.

Total

Suitability of School Plant:

1. It is pleasant to be in this building; it is kept clean and in good repair.

2. This school building has the space and physical arrangements needed to conduct the kinds of programs we have.

3. Students and staff are proud of their school plant and help to keep it attractive.

4. The grounds are attractive and provide adequate space for physical and recreational activities.		
5. School plant has appropriate facilities to carry out the curriculum goals.		
Total	☐	☐

Directions for Summarizing Data
on the CFK, Ltd., School Climate Profile

1. Separate questionnaires by role group (teachers, administrators, parents, students, etc.).
2. Compute sum of ratings given by each respondent for each category. Since there are five items per category, the maximum score would be 20, the minimum score 5.
3. Write this score in the box provided after item five in each category, both for "What Is" and for "What Should Be."
4. Since there is usually more than one respondent for each role group, compute the mean score for each category by adding all the scores for each category and dividing by the number of respondents. For example, suppose there are nine teacher questionnaires. Their scores on the General Climate Factor of "Respect" are as follows:

Teacher	"What Is" Score	"What Should Be" Score
1	15	19
2	13	20
3	18	20
4	18	20
5	11	18
6	17	20
7	14	20
8	12	19
9	15	19
	9/133	9/175
	14.8	19.4

5. Plot these mean scores (14.8 and 19.4) on the summary form using a solid black line for the "What Is" scores and a colored or broken line for the "What Should Be" scores. (See how to plot scores on sample summary form on page 70.)
6. Then compute in a similar manner the mean score for the other climate factors and plot them on the summary form as in Step 5.
7. Use a different summary form for each role group.
8. Later you may want to compare responses of particular role groups by plotting them on the same summary form, or by converting the summary into a transparency and superimposing the data for the two role groups one on the other.
9. It may be useful to summarize the data from all the role group respondents into one grand summary form. This will give a total picture of the school's climate. If the six role groups included 300 students, 50 teachers, 60 parents, 7 other staff, 4 building administrators, and 3 central office administrators, you could make the summary form by averaging the mean scores of each of these role groups, totaling their mean scores, and dividing by 6.

For example, using the general climate factor of "Respect" for "What Is," the mean scores for the six groups and the mean of all the groups can be computed as follows:

Role Group	Mean "What Is" Scores
1. Students	12.2
2. Teachers	15.4
3. Parents	12.3
4. Other staff	15.0
5. Building administrators	18.0
6. Central office administrators	17.2
	6/90.1
	15.0

This mean score of 15.0 for "What Is" with regard to "Respect" could then be plotted on the grand summary form.

The summary form on page 71 can be used to plot mean scores of various role group respondents for all climate factors and determinants.

Sample Summary Form
CFK, Ltd., School Climate Profile

General Climate Factors

For _____ School

Based on data summarized from _____ respondents.

(State role group)

A. General Climate Factors

1. Respect
2. Trust
3. High Morale
4. Opportunities for Input
5. Continuous Academic and Social Growth
6. Cohesiveness
7. School Renewal
8. Caring

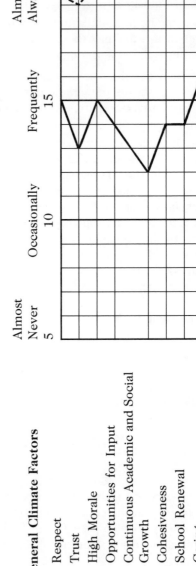

Note: *Solid line indicates mean "What Is" scores. Broken line indicates mean "What Should Be" scores.*

Summary Form of the CFK, Ltd., School Climate Profile

School: _____

Based on data summarized from _____ respondents.
(State role group)

	Almost Never 5	Occasionally 10	Frequently 15	Almost Always 20
A. General Climate Factors				
1. Respect				
2. Trust				
3. High Morale				
4. Opportunities for Input				
5. Continuous Academic and Social Growth				
6. Cohesiveness				
7. School Renewal				
8. Caring				
B. Program Determinants				
1. Opportunities for Active Learning				
2. Individualized Performance Expectations				
3. Varied Learning Environments				
4. Flexible Curriculum and Extracurricular Activities				
5. Support and Structure Appropriate to Learner's Maturity				
6. Rules Cooperatively Determined				
7. Varied Reward Systems				
C. Process Determinants				
1. Problem-Solving Ability				
2. Improvement of School Goals				
3. Identifying and Working with Conflicts				
4. Effective Communications				
5. Involvement in Decision Making				
6. Autonomy with Accountability				
7. Effective Teaching-Learning Strategies				
8. Ability to Plan for the Future				
D. Material Determinants				
1. Adequate Resources				
2. Supportive and Efficient Logistical System				
3. Suitability of School Plant				

Appendix C

Mini-Audit #1 and Mini-Audit #2
ACTIVITIES AND PROJECTS
FOR CLIMATE IMPROVEMENT

by Eugene Howard

General Information for Using Mini-Audits #1 and #2

Mini-Audit #1, designed to assess the program determinants of a school, will assist faculties and other leaders in identifying climate improvement priorities in the school and stimulate thoughtful discussion regarding activities, projects, and programs that affect a school's climate. Mini-Audit #2 assesses the process and material determinants of a school. Neither instrument is appropriate for research nor for comparison of one school with another.

The purpose of the mini-audit is to provide a faculty with a climate profile of a school. From this profile the faculty can identify some determinants that are strong and others that are comparatively weak. Activities, programs, and projects can then be designed to strengthen those determinants seen by the faculty as being potentially the most influential in improving the school's climate.

Respondents to the mini-audits may be staff members, mature, informed students, or parents who are well-acquainted with the school's programs and activities. It would not, however, be appropriate to ask people who have little knowledge of the school to complete the forms. For this reason we do not recommend giving the forms to all students or all parents.

Unlike other instruments, the two mini-audits are designed to assess the climate of a school in terms of specific activities, programs, and practices under way. The activities, programs, and practices identified are those that have been most often reported as being helpful in improving school climate.

These instruments are for your school. You may (and should) modify them by adding any activities, programs, or practices unique to your school, or change the wording of individual items to make them appropriate for your school. Do not drop items from the instrument simply because your school is not implementing the activity. Dropping such items might deprive you of important information regarding your faculty's attitude about new ideas you may wish to consider.

Some repetition of audit items may be noted. This repetition occurs because some activities, projects, and programs will, if working well, have an impact on more than one climate determinant.

Directions

What kinds of activities and projects are already under way in your school and are having a positive effect on your school's climate? The mini-audits are designed to help you define as many as possible. The mini-audits consist of a list of the most commonly identified activities and projects that relate to the various climate determinants.

Please rate each item on the basis of "What Is" (the extent to which the activity takes place in your school) and "What Should Be" (the extent to which you believe such an activity would influence your school's climate in a positive manner if it were operating well). Respond using the rating scale in the two boxes below.

What Is: the extent to which the activity takes place in your school.
1 = does not take place in this school.
2 = is in a beginning state of development. It operates on a very limited basis.
3 = is operating well but on a limited basis.
4 = is operating well on a schoolwide basis affecting most students in the school.

What Should Be: the extent to which the activity would influence the climate of the school positively if it were operating well on a schoolwide basis.
1 = would influence the school's climate negatively or not at all.
2 = would have a very limited positive effect on the school's climate.
3 = would have a positive effect on the school's climate.
4 = would have a very positive effect on the school's climate.

I am a: ☐ teacher
          ☐ other professional staff
          ☐ administrator
          ☐ student
          ☐ parent

Mini Audit #1 — Program Determinants

	What Is	What Should Be
A. Active Learning		

1. Use of manipulative materials in the classroom: models, machines, scales, live plants, measuring devices, scientific apparatus, blocks or rods for learning math, photographic and recording equipment.

1. _____   1. _____

2. Learning centers: areas within classrooms, laboratories, or media centers especially designed for learning activities such as creative writing, experimenting, dramatics, or learning games.

2. _____   2. _____

3. Use of the community as a classroom for active learning: interviewing, surveying opinions within the family or among neighbors, growing and observing plants or animals, field trips, learning projects in museums, attending concerts or art exhibits. For older pupils — internships in business or public agencies, work-study programs, community-based independent study programs.

3. _____   3. _____

4. Outdoor education activities related to regular in-school work: nature walks, supervised hiking, camping, map reading, collecting natural objects. For older pupils — outward bound-type programs, backpacking, conservation and science study, geological or archeological field trips.

4. _____   4. _____

5. Project work in school: designing and constructing useful things, making models, charts, maps, learning games, research projects, participating in school improve-

ment projects, building science fair-type projects, in-school independent study projects.

5. _____   5. _____

6. Use of games and simulations in the classroom.

6. _____   6. _____

7. Integration of the arts into the curriculum.

7. _____   7. _____

8. Multiculural active learning experiences: learning songs and dances of other cultures, learning words and phrases of other languages, eating food of other cultures, writing to pen pals, student exchange programs, videotape and art exchange programs, school-sponsored foreign travel.

8. _____   8. _____

9.

9. _____   9. _____

10.

10. _____   10. _____

Total

Mean Score

B. Individualized Performance Expectations/Varied Reward Systems

	What Is	What Should Be

1. Continuous progress curricula: students progress through the established curriculum at a rate appropriate to their ability and maturity. Performance expectations for pupils determined by ability and maturity.

1. _____   1. _____

2. Differentiated assignments: all students in the same class or learning group are not necessarily given the same assignments. Assignments vary depending on the student ability, interest, maturity, and previous achievement.

2. _____   2. _____

3. Learning contracts and independent study projects: plans for learning activities are in some cases mutually developed by learners and teachers. Performance expectations may be defined and agreed-on between the teacher and learner. In some cases, pupils contract for a grade (agree to complete certain activities or reach an

agreed-on level of competence in exchange for a specified grade).

4. Modifications of the grading system to reduce the negative effects of failure and over-competition: replacing or supplementing grades with lists of competencies demonstrated.

5. Expansion of the formal rewards system so that all students have an opportunity to be formally recognized by the school: expanding the honor roll to recognize more than academic achievement, "Student of the Week" recognition programs, "Thank-you grams" (notes thanking people for helping others), positive telephone calls home, reward buttons or pencils for work well done.

6.

7.

	3. _____	3. _____
	4. _____	4. _____
	5. _____	5. _____
	6. _____	6. _____
	7. _____	7. _____
Total	☐	☐
Mean Score	☐	☐

C. Varied Learning Environments, and Flexible Curriculum and Extracurricular Activities

| | What Is | What Should Be |

1. Learning environments outside the school: students are given assignments to be completed by using home or community resources; students initiate learning activities to utilize out-of-school resources. (Examples of out-of-school learning environments are home garden, farm, library, museum, concert hall, theater, office, factory, family trip, national park, bank, department store, or airport.)

1. _____   1. _____

2. Conventional classrooms modified so that a variety of learning environments is available within the room: the room offers a reading corner, an active learning center, an audiovisual area, and an independent study area; the room is designed for flexibili-

ty so that areas can be used for a variety of purposes.

2. _____   2. _____

3. A variety of types of learning areas available within the school: diagnostic and prescriptive learning areas, reading or language skills laboratories, media centers, areas designed for active learning, large-group instruction areas, areas designed for counseling, small-group work, and one-to-one teaching.

3. _____   3. _____

4. Opportunities for independent study: students, with teacher assistance, initiate, plan, and evaluate their own learning activities. Younger students are taught to assume responsibility for their own learning in accordance with their maturity.

4. _____   4. _____

5. Continuous progress curricula: students proceed through the established curriculum at an appropriate rate, and learning activities vary in accordance with the student's maturity and ability.

5. _____   5. _____

6. Career education programs, integrating career-related activities into the regular curriculum: students learn practical applications for academic skills and concepts, older pupils concentrate on careers of interest to them.

6. _____   6. _____

7. Artist or poet in the school programs.

7. _____   7. _____

8. The use of community resource persons to enrich the curriculum.

8. _____   8. _____

9. Special events cooperatively planned with community members and community organizations: community-school "interest days," art fairs, career days, "activities days," Junior Achievement activities, community-school service clubs.

9. _____   9. _____

10. Gifted and talented programs with learning activities especially planned for pupils with exceptional abilities in a variety of areas: academic achievement, fine and performing arts, leadership. Includes ad-

vanced study opportunities, mentorships, and internships.

	What Is	What Should Be
vanced study opportunities, mentorships, and internships.	10. _____	10. _____
11. An organized program to "involve the uninvolved" in the school's activities.	11. _____	11. _____
12. Scheduling of some activities during the school day to increase their availability to all pupils.	12. _____	12. _____
13. A noon-hour activities program.	13. _____	13. _____
14. A broad and diversified extracurricular program designed to appeal to pupils with a variety of interests and abilities.	14. _____	14. _____
15. A diversified intramurals program or, for younger pupils, supervised playground activities.	15. _____	15. _____
16.	16. _____	16. _____
17.	17. _____	17. _____
Total	☐	☐
Mean Score	☐	☐

D. Appropriate Support and Structure

	What Is	What Should Be
1. Well-staffed counseling: pupil personnel programs that serve individual student's needs.	1. _____	1. _____
2. Organized student support groups: for older students — peer counseling, peer tutoring, teacher advisor/advisee programs, group counseling. For younger students — "Magic Circle" or Glasser-type groups, group counseling.	2. _____	2. _____
3. Courses, units of study, or lessons designed to improve student self-concept, interpersonal relationships, self-understanding, conflict resolution, problem solving, and "how-to-study" skills.	3. _____	3. _____
4. Leadership training courses or units for students.	4. _____	4. _____
5. Special education programs of all types.	5. _____	5. _____

78

6. Big Brother/Big Sister programs and new
student orientation programs.   6. _____   6. _____

7. Effective, well-equipped, and well-stocked
instructional materials center to support ef-
fective instruction.   7. _____   7. _____

8.   8. _____   8. _____

9.   9. _____   9. _____

                              Total   [_____]   [_____]

                        Mean Score   [_____]   [_____]

		What
E. Rules Cooperatively Determined	**What Is**	**Should Be**

1. Student and staff involvement in writing
and publishing the student handbook.   1. _____   1. _____

2. Staff involvement in defining rules per-
taining to staff.   2. _____   2. _____

3. Student involvement in defining rules in
classrooms.   3. _____   3. _____

4.   4. _____   4. _____

5.   5. _____   5. _____

                              Total   [_____]   [_____]

                        Mean Score   [_____]   [_____]

Mini-Audit #2 —
Process and Material Determinants

Process Determinants

A. Problem Solving, Decision Making, and Resolving Conflicts	What Is	What Should Be

A. Problem Solving, Decision Making, and Resolving Conflicts

1. Problem-identification meetings or surveys: any procedures used to involve parents, students, staff, or others in identifying (not necessarily solving) problems related to your individual school.　　1. _____　1. _____

2. Teaching student leaders problem-solving processes: in the primary grades this may be done in "Magic Circle" or other group counseling-type sessions in which pupils resolve problems that occur within the class. Programs for older students may take the form of direct instruction in problem-solving skills for designated leaders such as student council members, class officers, or club officers.　　2. _____　2. _____

3. Task forces (parents, faculty, or students) working on school problems: task forces are working groups assigned the task of defining and resolving a problem, which has been identified as important through the problem-identification process.　　3. _____　3. _____

4. Faculty or student advisory groups to the principal to help with problem solving, decision making, or conflict resolution.　　4. _____　4. _____

5. Use of a formal decision-making model in decision-making groups such as departments, grade-level groups, faculty meetings, the student council, or the principal's administrative team. Models may include such components as: definition of the types of decisions that can be considered by the group, defining the group's membership, identifying who can vote or the method of arriving at consensus, and obligations of group members once a decision has been reached.　　5. _____　5. _____

6. School governance councils (groups with extensive decision-making and problem-solving responsibility): membership on such councils may be limited to professional staff members or may include student and parent representatives.

6. _____   6. _____

7. Conflict resolution committees: such committees are organized to identify growing conflicts among cliques or individuals and to resolve such conflicts before they become disruptive to the school.

7. _____   7. _____

8.

8. _____   8. _____

9.

9. _____   9. _____

Total

Mean Score

B. Improvement of School Goals and Planning for the Future

What Is | What Should Be

1. Student goals and objectives are identified as a part of the process for defining and articulating the curriculum. Such goals and objectives are in writing and are used as a basis for planning learning activities for students.

1. _____   1. _____

2. Through the school's program evaluation processes the strengths and weaknesses of each curriculum are periodically assessed. Information from such evaluations is used by the faculty to strengthen curricula in areas where weaknesses are identified.

2. _____   2. _____

3. Procedures have been established for involving parents, pupils, and staff in defining school improvement priorities.

3. _____   3. _____

4. A written plan exists for the improvement of the school. This plan identifies the school's priorities for improvement, identifies and assigns responsibility for improvement activities, and identifies target dates for completion of tasks.

4. _____   4. _____

5. Organizational units within the school, such as departments, teaching teams, or grade-level groups, develop and implement school improvement plans related to their areas of responsibility.   5. _____   5. _____

6. The staff evaluation system of the school encourages each individual staff member to develop instructional improvement objectives and to identify activities for achieving these objectives.   6. _____   6. _____

7.   7. _____   7. _____

Total

Mean Score

	What Is	What Should Be
C. Effective Communications		

1. Communications between the school and parents are facilitated through the use of newsletters, letters from the school, and letters from various programs within the school.   1. _____   1. _____

2. Parents have opportunities to communicate with teachers informally by attending a variety of school-sponsored activities: parent orientation programs, school performances, sports events, back-to-school nights, dramatic and art activities, or art fairs.   2. _____   2. _____

3. Communication between parents and the school administration and faculty is facilitated through a parent volunteer program.   3. _____   3. _____

4. Parents learn about their children's achievements in school through a "positive calls home" or a "positive letters home" program.   4. _____   4. _____

5. Parents, faculty members, and individual students meet periodically to discuss the student's progress through a parent-student conferencing program.   5. _____   5. _____

6. Parents attend parenting classes or parent effectiveness training programs as a means of communicating with the school about problems they are having with their children.

6. _____   6. _____

7. A PTA or similar organization functions to keep communications open between the home and the school.

7. _____   7. _____

8. Parents and other community members communicate with the school by participating in community-sponsored events that use school facilities.

8. _____   8. _____

9. The principal periodically invites parents to meet with him/her to discuss school programs, plans, and problems (a "coffee klatch" day).

9. _____   9. _____

10. Administrators and faculty members facilitate informal communication between school and community by participating in community organizations and attending community-sponsored events.

10. _____   10. _____

11. The school organizes retreats designed to open communications among staff members, among students, and between staff and students.

11. _____   11. _____

12. Faculty meetings are planned so that they provide for communication-opening activities among faculty members and between the faculty and administration.

12. _____   12. _____

13. The social structure (clique structure) of the school is studied and activities are planned to open communications among various cliques that are isolated from one another.

13. _____   13. _____

14.

14. _____   14. _____

15.

15. _____   15. _____

Total

Mean Score

D. Autonomy with Accountability

	What Is	What Should Be

1. Task forces assume responsibility for working on school improvement activities or projects.

1. _____   1. _____

2. Faculty planning committees develop plans for school improvement.

2. _____   2. _____

3. Student organizations (service or special interest clubs, student council) assume responsibility for operating portions of the school's activities program that have been delegated to them.

3. _____   3. _____

4. School service clubs assume responsibility for school and community improvement projects.

4. _____   4. _____

5. Through student volunteer programs, pupils assume responsibility for helping others in the school or the community. (Examples: younger children serve as teacher helpers, peer tutors, or library aides; older pupils serve as peer tutors or counselors, big brothers or big sisters, or volunteer to work in hospitals or retirement homes).

5. _____   5. _____

6. Students assume responsibility for planning and evaluating some of their own learning by participating in independent study programs.

6. _____   6. _____

7. Students assume responsibility for improving their own behavior through behavior contracts. (Behavior contracts are written agreements between a pupil and staff member in which pupils agree to modify their behavior. Parents, other staff members, or other pupils may help.)

7. _____   7. _____

8.

8. _____   8. _____

9.

9. _____   9. _____

Total

Mean Score

E. Effective Teaching/Learning Strategies

	What Is	What Should Be

1. Teachers use a variety of sub-grouping strategies within classrooms and laboratories: interest groups, project groups, tutorial groups, research groups, learning teams, fact-gathering groups, creative writing groups, groups with members who have common learning needs, discussion groups.

1. _____ 1. _____

2. Students plan their own work and participate in their own evaluation through a variety of independent study programs.

2. _____ 2. _____

3. Teachers provide students with prompt feedback regarding the quality of their work as they engage in learning tasks.

3. _____ 3. _____

4. Teachers organize learning activities in such a way that students are encouraged to learn from one another and help one another.

4. _____ 4. _____

5. Teachers use differentiated assignments as a means of providing for individual differences in learning styles, interest, beliefs, and maturity. All individuals in a class do not necessarily receive the same assignment.

5. _____ 5. _____

6. Teachers recognize that the "time on task" needed to master a given objective will vary among students; therefore, teachers organize their instruction in such a way that some students may take longer to master an objective than others.

6. _____ 6. _____

7. Teachers and students use the materials available in the school library or media center as a means of enriching the curriculum, providing for individual differences, and increasing motivation.

7. _____ 7. _____

8. A variety of active learning activities are planned: experimenting, working with real objects, simulating, model building, opinion surveying, designing and constructing, observing plants and animals, or collecting natural objects.

8. _____ 8. _____

9. Teachers systematically use diagnostic and prescriptive techniques to determine learning needs of individual pupils and assign learning tasks related to those needs.

9. _____   9. _____

10.   10. _____   10. _____

11.   11. _____   11. _____

Total   [ ]   [ ]

Mean Score   [ ]   [ ]

Material Determinants

	What Is	**What Should Be**
A. Adequate Resources		

1. Learning materials and equipment in individual classrooms are adequate.

1. _____   1. _____

2. Learning materials and equipment in such areas as gyms, labs, shops, and music areas are adequate.

2. _____   2. _____

3. A well-equipped library/media center provides a wide variety of books, magazines, manipulative materials, and audiovisual materials and equipment.

3. _____   3. _____

4. Community resources, both human and material, are used by learners as a part of their regular program.

4. _____   4. _____

5. The materials and supply budget to teachers is adequate to encourage teacher creativity.

5. _____   5. _____

6.   6. _____   6. _____

7.   7. _____   7. _____

Total   [ ]   [ ]

Mean Score   [ ]   [ ]

B. Supportive and Efficient Logistical Systems	**What Is**	**What Should Be**

1. A well-organized district warehouse supplies materials and equipment on demand.

1. _____   1. _____

2. Procedures exist for quickly authorizing purchases for materials and supplies and for prompt delivery.

2. _____   2. _____

3. Provisions have been made for reimbursing teachers for materials bought by them for use in their work with students.

3. _____   3. _____

4. A local or regional film library fills orders efficiently and promptly.

4. _____   4. _____

5. Equipment needed for instruction can be repaired promptly and efficiently.

5. _____   5. _____

6.

6. _____   6. _____

Total

Mean Score

C. Suitability of School Plant	What Is	What Should Be
1. School plant flexibility is encouraged by providing folding or movable partitions.	1. _____	1. _____
2. The school plant provides variable-size learning areas to accommodate different kinds of learning/teaching groups.	2. _____	2. _____
3. A variety of types of furniture is provided in the school plant.	3. _____	3. _____
4. The school plant is attractive and aesthetically pleasing; for example: murals, plants, carpeting.	4. _____	4. _____
5. Temperature and light controls are well designed.	5. _____	5. _____
6. Provision is made for keeping the building and grounds clean at all times.	6. _____	6. _____
7. Grounds are attractively landscaped and carefully planned to accommodate a variety of learning activities.	7. _____	7. _____
8. The school site has been extended to include a school farm or outdoor education camp.	8. _____	8. _____

9.   9. _____   9. _____

Total ☐ ☐

Mean Score ☐ ☐

Summarizing the Results

Follow these steps to summarize the results of the mini-audits:

1. Separate the questionnaires by role groups.

2. Compute the average (mean) rating given by each respondent for each determinant.

3. Enter these figures in the boxes provided on the questionnaire.

4. Since there is more than one respondent for each role group, compute the mean score for each category (determinant) by adding all the scores for each category and dividing by the number of respondents.

5. Plot these mean scores on a blank summary form. (See sample of completed summary form on page 90.) The column titled "Number of Activities Identified and Verified" is left blank at this point. It means that the activity has been identified by respondents as taking place in the school. Information for this column will come from the item analysis.

6. After computing in a similar manner the mean scores for each category of climate determinant, connect the "What Is" scores with a black line. Then connect the "What Should Be" scores with a red or a broken line.

7. Use a different summary form for each role group. Possible role groups include teachers, counselors and other specialists, administrators, members of the Climate Improvement Committee, students, parents.

8. Later you may want to compare responses of particular role groups by plotting them on the same summary form or by converting the summary form into a transparency and superimposing the data of one role group over another.

Preparing an Item Analysis

During the meeting at which the results of the mini-audit are to be discussed, the faculty will need to refer to the original items in the audit. Results can best be reported in graphic form by plotting the average of all responses for each item, as illustrated in the Sample Item Analysis Report Form on page 91. After plotting the data on these forms, you may reproduce them for distribution to the respondents or make them into overhead transparencies for communicating the results to your faculty and other groups. Item Analysis Report Forms for Mini-Audits #1 and #2 are included at the end of this Appendix.

After you have plotted the "What Is" and "What Should Be" lines on the item analysis sheets, count the number of activities that have been rated 2.0 or more in the "What Is" column. You may consider these items as "verified"; that is, they are happening at least to some extent in your school. Count the number of verified activities and record it in the space provided at the end of each section of the Item Analysis Report Form. Then enter it in the column on the summary form.

Interpreting the Item Analysis

In interpreting the results of your item analysis, the following questions are useful:

1. Which activities or projects are least developed in your school? (In the sample they would be items 2, 3, 5, 6, and 8 — all rated under 2.0.)

2. Which activities or projects in the "What Should Be" ratings are seen as having the greatest potential for making a positive impact on your school's climate? (In the sample they would be items 4, 7, 9 and 10 — all rated above 2.0.) Perhaps the faculty should consider a project to increase these activities in the school.

3. Which activities or projects are most developed in your school? (Items 4, 9, and 10.) What could be done to strengthen these activities?

4. Which of the items are rated by the faculty as having the lowest potential for positively affecting the school's climate? (Items 2 and 3.) Does this mean that the faculty should spend less time in developing these activities than in developing others?

5. In which climate determinants have the faculty identified and verified the most activities? In which determinant areas have they identified the fewest activities? Should the faculty consider launching additional activities to strengthen determinant areas in which not much is happening?

Sample Completed Summary Form

Activities and Projects that Affect Climate Positively

School _____
Role Group _____
No. of Respondents _____

Determinants	Number of Activities Identified & Verified	Mean Ratings
		What Is (1, 2) — What Should Be (3, 4)
A. Active Learning		
B. Individualized Performance Expectations/Varied Reward Systems		
C. Varied Learning Environments Flexible Curriculum & Extra-curricular Activities		
D. Appropriate Support & Structure		
E. Rules Cooperatively Determined		

Sample Item Analysis Report Form

School _____

Date _____

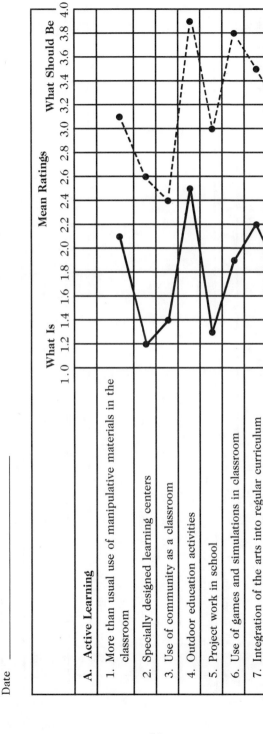

Number of identified and verified activities (2.0 or more on the "What is" scale): _____

Item Analysis Report Form
Mini-Audit #1

Program Determinants

	What Is Mean Ratings															What Should Be					
	1.0	1.2	1.4	1.6	1.8	2.0	2.2	2.4	2.6	2.8	3.0	3.2	3.4	3.6	3.8	4.0
A. Active Learning																
1. More than usual use of manipulative materials in the classroom																
2. Specially designed learning centers																
3. Use of community as a classroom																
4. Outdoor education activities																
5. Project work in school																
6. Use of games and simulations in classroom																
7. Integration of the arts into regular curriculum																
8. Multi-cultural active learning experiences																
9.																
10.																

Number of identified and verified activities (2.0 or more on the "What is" scale): _____

Mean Ratings

	What Is								2.6	2.8	3.0	3.2	What Should Be			
	1.0	1.2	1.4	1.6	1.8	2.0	2.2	2.4	2.6	2.8	3.0	3.2	3.4	3.6	3.8	4.0
B. Individualized Performance Expectations/Varied Reward Systems																
1. Continuous progress curricula																
2. Differentiated assignments																
3. Learning contracts and independent study projects																
4. Modifications of the grading system																
5. Expanding rewards system																
6.																
7.																

Number of identified and verified activities (2.0 or more on the "What is" scale): _____

Mean Ratings

	What Is								2.6	2.8	3.0	3.2	What Should Be			
	1.0	1.2	1.4	1.6	1.8	2.0	2.2	2.4	2.6	2.8	3.0	3.2	3.4	3.6	3.8	4.0
C. Varied Learning Environments/Flexible Curriculum and Extracurricular Activities																
1. Use of learning environments outside the school																

	Mean Ratings															
	What Is							What Should Be								
	1.0	1.2	1.4	1.6	1.8	2.0	2.2	2.4	2.6	2.8	3.0	3.2	3.4	3.6	3.8	4.0
2. Modification of conventional classrooms																
3. Variety of learning areas within the school																
4. Opportunities for independent study																
5. Continuous progress curricula																
6. Integrating career-related activities into the regular curriculum																
7. Artist or poet in the school programs																
8. Use of community resource persons to enrich the curriculum																
9. Special events planned with community																
10. Gifted and talented programs																
11. "Involve the uninvolved" programs																
12. Increase availability of activities during the school day																
13. A noon-hour activities program																
14. Diversified extracurricular program to appeal to a variety of individuals																

	Mean Ratings															
	What Is											**What Should Be**				
	1.0	1.2	1.4	1.6	1.8	2.0	2.2	2.4	2.6	2.8	3.0	3.2	3.4	3.6	3.8	4.0
15. Diversified intramurals program or supervised playground activities																
16.																
17.																

Number of identified and verified activities (2.0 or more on the "What is" scale): _____

	Mean Ratings															
	What Is											**What Should Be**				
	1.0	1.2	1.4	1.6	1.8	2.0	2.2	2.4	2.6	2.8	3.0	3.2	3.4	3.6	3.8	4.0
D. Appropriate Support and Structure																
1. Well-staffed counseling — pupil personnel programs																
2. Organized student support groups																
3. Courses, units of study, or lesson plans for self-concept, etc.																
4. Leadership training for students																
5. Special education program																
6. Big Brother/Big Sister programs and new student orientation																

95

	What Is											Mean Ratings											What Should Be
---	1.0	1.2	1.4	1.6	1.8	2.0	2.2	2.4	2.6	2.8	3.0	3.2	3.4	3.6	3.8	4.0
7. Effective instructional materials center																
8.																
9.																

Number of identified and verified activities (2.0 or more on the "What is" scale): _____

	What Is											Mean Ratings											What Should Be
---	1.0	1.2	1.4	1.6	1.8	2.0	2.2	2.4	2.6	2.8	3.0	3.2	3.4	3.6	3.8	4.0
E. Rules Cooperatively Determined																
1. Student and staff involvement in writing and publishing the student handbook																
2. Staff involvement in defining rules pertaining to staff																
3. Student involvement in defining rules in classroom																
4.																
5.																

Number of identified and verified activities (2.0 or more on the "What is" scale): _____

Item Analysis Report Form
Mini-Audit #2

Process Determinants

	Mean Ratings															
	What Is										What Should Be					
	1.0	1.2	1.4	1.6	1.8	2.0	2.2	2.4	2.6	2.8	3.0	3.2	3.4	3.6	3.8	4.0
A. Problem Solving/Decision Making and Resolving Conflicts																
1. Problem-identification meetings or surveys																
2. Teaching student leaders problem-solving processes																
3. Task forces																
4. Faculty or student advisory groups to the principal																
5. Use of a formal decision-making model in decision-making groups																
6. School governance councils																
7. Conflict resolution committees																
8.																
9.																
B. Improvement of School Goals and Planning for the Future																
1. Student goals and objectives identified and are in writing																

	Mean Ratings															
	What Is												What Should Be			
	1.0	1.2	1.4	1.6	1.8	2.0	2.2	2.4	2.6	2.8	3.0	3.2	3.4	3.6	3.8	4.0
2. Strengths and weaknesses of school program assessed periodically																
3. Procedures established for involving parents in defining priorities																
4. Written plan identifying school's priorities for improvement																
5. Organizational units within the school develop plans related to their area of responsibility																
6. Staff evaluation encourages staff to develop instructional improvement																
7.																
C Effective Communications																
1. Communications between school and parents facilitated by various programs within the school																
2. Teacher/parent communication through informal school-sponsored activities																
3. Communications between parents, school administration, and faculty facilitated through parent volunteer program.																

Mean Ratings

Item	1.0	1.2	1.4	1.6	1.8	2.0	2.2	2.4	2.6	2.8	3.0	3.2	3.4	3.6	3.8	4.0
	What Is													What Should Be		
4. Children's achievements learned about through various programs																
5. Periodic meetings to discuss pupil's progress																
6. Parents attend training programs as a means of communicating about problems with their children																
7. PTA keeps communications open between home and school																
8. Community members communicate with school by participating in community-sponsored events																
9. Principal periodically invites parents to meet informally with him/her																
10. Administrators and faculty members participate in community-sponsored events																
11. School organizes retreats designed to open communications among staff and students																
12. Faculty meetings planned to provide communication-opening activities among faculty and administrators																
13. Social structure of school studied to open communications among various cliques																

	Mean Ratings															
	What Is									What Should Be						
	1.0	1.2	1.4	1.6	1.8	2.0	2.2	2.4	2.6	2.8	3.0	3.2	3.4	3.6	3.8	4.0
14.																
15.																
D. Autonomy with Accountability																
1. Task forces assume responsibility for working on school improvement projects																
2. Faculty planning committees develop plans for school improvement																
3. Student organizations assume responsibility for school activities delegated to them																
4. School service clubs assume responsibility for school and community improvement projects																
5. Students in volunteer programs assume responsibility for helping others																
6. Students assume responsibility for independent study programs																
7. Student behavior contracts																
8.																
9.																

Mean Ratings

	What Is											What Should Be				
	1.0	1.2	1.4	1.6	1.8	2.0	2.2	2.4	2.6	2.8	3.0	3.2	3.4	3.6	3.8	4.0
E. Effective Teaching/Learning Strategies																
1. Teachers use of sub-grouping strategies																
2. Pupil independent study programs																
3. Prompt feedback by teachers regarding pupils' work																
4. Activities organized by teachers encourage students to help one another																
5. Differentiated assignments for individual differences in learning styles																
6. Teachers recognize "time on task" needed to master given objective will vary among pupils																
7. Use of materials available in school library																
8. Learning activities planned to encourage involvement of pupils in a variety of active learning activities																
9. Teachers use diagnostic techniques to determine learning needs																
10.																
11.																

Material Determinants

	Mean Ratings	
	What Is	What Should Be
	1.0 1.2 1.4 1.6 1.8 2.0 2.2 2.4 2.6 2.8 3.0	3.2 3.4 3.6 3.8 4.0

A. Adequate Resources

1. Adequate learning materials and equipment in individual classrooms

2. Adequate learning materials and equipment in such areas as gyms, labs, shops, and music areas

3. A well-equipped library and media center provides a wide variety of books, magazines, manipulative materials, and audiovisual materials and equipment

4. Use of community resources (both human and material) by learner

5. Materials and supply budget adequate to encourage teacher creativity

6.

7.

B. Supportive and Efficient Logistical Systems

1. A well-organized district warehouse supplies materials and equipment on demand

	Mean Ratings															
	What Is						What Should Be									
	1.0	1.2	1.4	1.6	1.8	2.0	2.2	2.4	2.6	2.8	3.0	3.2	3.4	3.6	3.8	4.0
2. Procedures exist for quickly authorizing purchases for materials and supplies and for prompt delivery																
3. Provisions have been made for reimbursing teachers for materials bought by them for use in their work with pupils																
4. A local or regional film library fills orders efficiently and promptly																
5. Equipment needed for instruction can be repaired quickly and efficiently																
6.																
C. Suitability of School Plant																
1. School plant flexibility is encouraged through provision of folding or demountable partitions																
2. The school plant provides learning areas of a variety of sizes to accommodate different kinds of learning-teaching groups																
3. A variety of types of furniture is provided in the school plant																
4. The school plant is attractive and aesthetically pleasing; murals, plants, carpeting																

| | Mean Ratings | | | | | | | | | | | | | | | |
| | What Is | | | | | | | | | What Should Be | | | | | |
	1.0	1.2	1.4	1.6	1.8	2.0	2.2	2.4	2.6	2.8	3.0	3.2	3.4	3.6	3.8	4.0
5. Temperature and light controls are well designed																
6. Provision is made for keeping the building and grounds clean at all times																
7. Grounds are attractively landscaped and carefully planned to accommodate a variety of learning activities																
8. The school site has been extended to include a school farm or outdoor education camp																

Appendix D
Brainstorming and Prioritizing Activity Instruction Sheet

Objective

The purpose of this activity is to identify from five to ten promising activities, projects, or programs that might be implemented to improve the climate of a school.

Use of the Information

The recommendations for climate improvement activities made by the group will be used for planning activities to follow up the climate survey.

Procedure

1. *Structuring (5 minutes).* Appoint a leader and a recorder for the group.

2. *Some Ideas for Your Group (5 minutes).* Give the group a one-page list of possible activities that have been used by other faculties to strengthen the climate determinant the group will discuss. This list is intended to stimulate the group's thinking regarding how this climate determinant might be strengthened in this school. Make it clear that the activities listed are not intended as recommendations for implementation in this school. Ask the group to read the list of activities as examples of what might be done.

3. *Brainstorming (25 minutes).* Read the "Rules for Brainstorming" to the group (see below). Then ask the group members to think of as many ideas as they can for strengthening the climate determinants the group has been assigned to consider. The group may wish to consider strengthening some activities, programs, and projects already under way in the school as well as implementing new activities. Refer to the results of the climate survey to identify what is already going on in the school.

Instruct the recorder to list all ideas offered on a large sheet of paper posted where all can see it. Tell the group it will have 20 minutes to list as many ideas as possible.

4. *Prioritizing (10 minutes).* Explain to the group that it should recommend from five to ten of the most promising ideas that have been listed. Ideas recommended should be those the group feels have the greatest potential for influencing the school climate positively. When the group has reached agreement on an idea, instruct the recorder to place a large star in front of that idea on the large sheet of paper.

5. *Reporting (20 minutes).* Ask the group leader to give a report on the group's recommendations to the total faculty. Remind the group leader to limit the report to only the priority recommendations. Allow about two minutes for each group's report.

Rules for Brainstorming

1. Anyone can contribute ideas, but only one person talks at a time.
2. Give the group recorder enough time to write down one idea before offering another.
3. It is strictly against the rules to criticize or otherwise discuss an idea. Discussion comes later, after all the ideas are presented.
4. Remember that what is desired is quantity of ideas, not quality. Offer your idea even if you do not think it is a very good one. Your "wild" idea may trigger a not-so-wild idea from someone else. Any idea is of value.
5. Piggyback or combine ideas. Not only should you come up with ideas but you also should be alert to ways to add or improve on another person's idea.